I0447769

Distribution and Migration of North American Ducks, Geese and Swans

by Wells W. Cooke

with an introduction by Jackson Chambers

This work contains material that was originally published in 1906.

This publication is within the Public Domain.

*This edition is reprinted for educational purposes
and in accordance with all applicable Federal Laws.*

Introduction Copyright 2016 by Jackson Chambers

Introduction

I am pleased to present yet another title in the Waterfowl series.

This volume is entitled "Distribution and Migration of North American Ducks, Geese and Swans" and was published in 1906.

The work is in the Public Domain and is re-printed here in accordance with Federal Laws.

Though this work is a century old it contains much information on poultry that is still pertinent today.

As with all reprinted books of this age that are intended to perfectly reproduce the original edition, considerable pains and effort had to be undertaken to correct fading and sometimes outright damage to existing proofs of this title. At times, this task is quite monumental, requiring an almost total "rebuilding" of some pages from digital proofs of multiple copies. Despite this, imperfections still sometimes exist in the final proof and may detract from the visual appearance of the text.

I hope you enjoy reading this book as much as I enjoyed making it available to readers again.

Jackson Chambers

Nat Hist.

LETTER OF TRANSMITTAL.

U. S. DEPARTMENT OF AGRICULTURE,
BIOLOGICAL SURVEY,
Washington, D. C., July 10, 1906.

SIR: I have the honor to transmit herewith, for publication as Bulletin No. 26 of the Biological Survey, a report on the Distribution and Migration of North American Ducks, Geese, and Swans, by Wells W. Cooke, assistant in the Biological Survey. Formerly abundant over the whole of the United States, waterfowl are steadily diminishing in numbers, and some species appear to be threatened with extinction in the not distant future. Their value for food is great, and they have formed in the past, and for all future time should continue to form, a valuable asset and an important source of revenue to the several States which harbor them. The preservation of the numerous species of ducks, geese, and swans is becoming an important matter of legislative enactment, and the present report is intended to furnish information as to present range, abundance, and migration of the several species with reference to practical legislation.

Respectfully,

H. W. HENSHAW,
Acting Chief, Biological Survey.

Hon. JAMES WILSON,
Secretary of Agriculture.

3

CONTENTS.

DISTRIBUTION AND MIGRATION OF NORTH AMERICAN DUCKS, GEESE, AND SWANS.

INTRODUCTION.

Wild fowl are distributed over the whole world. From time immemorial ducks, geese, and swans have been held in high esteem by mankind, and everywhere they have been eagerly pursued for sport or for food.

Passing by the purely esthetic value of the birds as beautiful and welcome denizens of our waters and as lending the charm of life and animation to our otherwise desolate ponds and lakes; passing by, too, their importance to thousands of men who are lured from business cares to pursue them and who derive from their pursuit both health and pleasure, their economic value and importance as food are very great. The flesh not only is palatable and nutritious, but is so different from that of domestic fowls as to form a most welcome addition to the table both of the rich and the poor.

The flesh of wild fowl constituted an important item in the larder of the aborigines of this country, who, by means of the bow and arrow and by the use of various devices in the shape of nets and traps, succeeded in obtaining them in considerable numbers, especially when young and unable to fly. The Eskimo and northern Indians, indeed, would fare badly but for the vast numbers of waterfowl that visit their country to breed, and everywhere the aborigines seek their eggs with avidity. Waterfowl as an addition to the larder became almost as essential to the first settlers as they had been to the Indians, and, so far as game was concerned, the fowling piece soon became a more important part of the settler's equipment than the rifle.

Neither the aborigines nor the early settlers appreciably reduced the numbers of the hordes of ducks and geese that periodically covered the lakes, ponds, rivers, and marshes of this favored country. It was not until comparatively recent times, indeed, that the tremendous increase of population and the constantly increasing number both of sportsmen and of market gunners, together with the invention of that potent engine of destruction, the breech-loading gun, have had their logical effect in greatly diminishing their numbers and in practically exterminating not a few species.

So rapidly are some species diminishing in numbers in certain States that the market supply is already threatened, and Minnesota has found it necessary to pass laws prohibiting not only the export of ducks, but even their sale within the State limits. Such radical legislation in a State where only a few years since waterfowl abounded on every lake and waterway, reveals how imminent is the danger and how pressing the value and importance of prohibitive laws, and it becomes evident that if any considerable number of waterfowl are to be preserved, spring shooting must be abolished and the sale of wild fowl limited to the States where killed.

The enforcement of moderately stringent protective laws, however, and the establishment of preserves in the States where waterfowl can be sure of shelter and safety, are likely to result not only in averting the threatened extinction of certain species, but in the increase of all waterfowl to a point somewhere near their recent abundance. Should the lessons of the past be unheeded and protection be withheld for a few years, then measures of the most radical kind will be necessary.

Of the 64 species and subspecies of ducks, geese, and swans which occur in North America north of Mexico, 24 breed in the United States. The species most important to us are the wood duck, mallard, black duck, teal, canvasback, redhead, and Canada goose. Several of these species breed only in the Northern States; but the cinnamon teal and ruddy duck nest as far south as southern California, and the wood duck breeds almost everywhere throughout the United States, and, moreover, the great bulk of this species winters within our boundaries.

It is a sad commentary on our present system of game protection that the wood duck, one of the handsomest of our native birds and one whose breeding range is almost entirely within our boundaries, is the species which has suffered most. So persistently has this duck been pursued that in some sections it has been practically exterminated. Even in States in which it still breeds commonly, as in Delaware and Maryland on the Atlantic coast and in Illinois in the Mississippi Valley, public sentiment fails to recognize the importance of adequately protecting the bird, and the laws still permit it to be destroyed late in the spring. As a result the wood duck is constantly diminishing in numbers, and soon is likely to be known only from books or by tradition.

PROTECTION.

Wherever waterfowl already breed, or where the conditions are such as to favor their remaining during the summer, every effort should be made to increase the number of breeding birds by adequate protection both in the spring and during the nesting season, and, wherever possible, game refuges or preserves suitable for breeding purposes should be established.

Protective laws intended to shorten the open seasons, to prohibit spring shooting, eliminate destructive methods of hunting, and to stop sale and export have often provoked opposition from those who maintain that it is futile to attempt the protection of migratory birds in the North if they are not equally well protected on their winter feeding grounds in the South.

Recent experience, however, shows that under certain circumstances the results of local protection are immediate and very striking. In the San Luis Valley, Colorado, protection afforded ducks within an inclosure about an artificial pond, fed by an artesian well, has caused the birds to resort to the pond in increasing numbers each winter. At Palm Beach, Fla., where no hunting is allowed within a mile of the town, ducks have become so tame that they will come within a few feet for food, while outside the mile limit the same birds are so wild that it is difficult to approach them within gunshot. In Jefferson County, N. Y., the enactment of a local law prohibiting spring shooting has resulted in several species remaining to breed which formerly went much farther north to lay their eggs, when continually harassed by constant hunting in the spring. The enactment of a State law in New York prohibiting the shooting and sale of ducks and geese in spring has not only had a marked effect on local birds, but has resulted also in extending protection to waterfowl in North Carolina by restricting in the latter State their slaughter for the markets of New York City.

These and other illustrations which might readily be cited show that, if protected, many species that formerly reared their young in the United States, and were driven away by persecution, would return and occupy old breeding grounds. They prove also that very effective work for the protection and increase of waterfowl can be done in many sections of the country without waiting for general legislation or for concerted action on the part of the Southern States. Cooperative legislation on the part of the Southern States is greatly to be desired and may be expected to follow as the causes that have led to the diminution in the numbers of waterfowl are better understood there and as the purpose and effects of protective legislation in Northern States are fully comprehended.

With reference to practical legislation in behalf of wild fowl, questions often arise as to the time when various species may be expected at certain points in the autumn, when they leave for their breeding grounds in the spring, how late in the season shooting can be continued without interfering with pairing, what progress in legislation has been made in different parts of the United States, and what have been the practical results of such legislation.

In order to enable the Department to answer such inquiries, a comprehensive investigation of the general facts relating to our wild fowl has been undertaken. In the present report are presented such data as are now available respecting the distribution and migration of the ducks, geese, brant, and swans of North America, together with a brief reference to a few species which occur in Panama and the West Indies. A summary is also given of existing information as to the breeding grounds occupied by the several species, their winter resorts, the routes selected in passing north and south, and the times of making their journeys. Other subjects of investigation still under way are the food habits of the various species, principal ducking grounds, methods of hunting, and the means which have thus far proved most successful in the protection of these birds.

The problem of the legal protection of ducks, geese, and swans has two phases—protection during the breeding season and protection during migration and in winter. The first phase concerns 24 species of ducks breeding in the United States, while 46 species come under the head of winter residents of the United States. It happens, however, that from the economic point of view the 24 species of ducks and geese that breed in the United States comprise the most important North American species; among this number also are all the species that at the present time need protection while breeding. Of the 24 species, 5 are numerically unimportant and are confined to the southern portions of the United States and southward, so that they are of little importance for the market and as objects of sport. These 5 are the Florida duck, mottled duck, masked duck, black-bellied tree-duck, and fulvous tree-duck.

The other 19 species that breed regularly and commonly in the United States are as follows:

American merganser, *Merganser americanus.*
Hooded merganser, *Lophodytes cucullatus.*
Mallard, *Anas boschas.*
Black duck, *Anas obscura.*
Gadwall, *Chaulelasmus streperus.*
Baldpate, *Mareca americana.*
Green-winged teal, *Nettion carolinense.*
Blue-winged teal, *Querquedula discors.*
Cinnamon teal, *Querquedula cyanoptera.*
Shoveler, *Spatula clypeata.*
Pintail, *Dafila acuta.*
Wood duck, *Aix sponsa.*
Redhead, *Aythya americana.*
Canvasback, *Aythya vallisneria.*
Lesser scaup, *Aythya affinis.*
Ring-necked duck, *Aythya collaris.*
Ruddy duck, *Erismatura jamaicensis.*
Canada goose, *Branta canadensis.*
White-cheeked goose, *Branta canadensis occidentalis.*

A glance shows that this list comprises the species that in later years have decreased most in numbers, and hence that most need protection.

CAUSES OF DECREASE IN NUMBERS OF WATERFOWL.

The principal causes of the diminished numbers of waterfowl have been market hunting, spring shooting, and the destruction of the breeding grounds for farming purposes. Previous to twenty years ago, market hunting was the principal factor in the steady diminution of waterfowl. Since 1885, however, the problem of duck preservation in North America has entirely changed. The prairie districts of central Canada, comprising large portions of Manitoba, Saskatchewan, and Alberta are the "ducks' paradise." Within the United States this favored region extends to the northeastern part of Montana, the northern half of North Dakota, and the northwestern corner of Minnesota. The whole vast region is crowded with lakes, ponds, sloughs, and marshes that furnish ideal nesting conditions and unlimited food. Forty years ago every available nook was crowded . with waterfowl, and the whole region, 200 miles wide by 400 miles in length, was a great breeding colony, and numbered its inhabitants by the hundreds of thousands. To the northward the forests formed a partial boundary; to the southward, the general absence of suitable breeding grounds was the controlling factor, restricting the breeding waterfowl to the few lakes and marshes. The number of breeding ducks decreased rapidly from central North Dakota southward, until the outposts were reached in the lake region of southern Wisconsin, the Kankakee marshes of Illinois and Indiana, a few favored spots in southwestern Minnesota, and the lakes of north-central Iowa. In southern Wisconsin in 1864, every pond hole and every damp depression had its brood of young ducks. During the next fifteen years the farming of the region changed from grain raising to dairying, the marshes were drained, the former duck nurseries became grazing grounds, and duck hunting there was a sport of the past.

An article written in 1877 on the birds of northeastern Illinois enumerates 12 species of ducks as breeding commonly in the vicinity and 3 others as occasionally found there in summer. At present, a brood of young ducks in this region is rare. In 1885 some 14 species bred near Clear Lake, Iowa, and 16 species at Heron Lake, Minnesota. Now scarcely any ducks breed at either lake. But the places just mentioned were merely the outskirts of the " ducks' paradise." As great a change has taken place in the very heart of the breeding grounds. The Northern Pacific Railroad cut across its southern border in Minnesota and North Dakota and this was soon followed by a north and south line to Winnipeg. Other shorter branches were built later, but the final doom of the ducks was apparent when the Canadian Pacific Railroad crossed between Winnipeg and the Rocky Mountains the finest duck breeding grounds on the continent. During the past decade, the last stronghold of the waterfowl has been invaded, and soon the great breeding colonies of northern Alberta and Saskatchewan will be of the past. The population of North Dakota increased many fold from 1880 to 1900, and during this same period the vast prairies of central Canada were changed to wheat fields. It is evident, therefore, that in the United States and southern Canada in a few years there will be no great breeding colonies of the ducks most valued for sport and for the table. The future supply must come from isolated pairs and small colonies scattered in favorable localities over Canada and the northern quarter of the United States. Fortunately, such favorable places exist and will continue to exist for many years.

An important question in connection with the protection of ducks is the time when they pair for the breeding season, since it is evident that if shooting is continued after the birds are paired a decided decrease in the number of broods will result. While the present state of knowledge does not warrant positive statements as to the exact date of pairing of each species, enough has been learned to show that in the case of many species pairing occurs before the breeding grounds are reached. Many if not most of the mallards and shovelers that pass through Illinois on their way to more northern breeding grounds are paired before they leave that State, and the same is true of these species in Iowa. Many black ducks, wood ducks, and teal are paired in the spring by the time they reach Massachusetts. The following letter from Hon. John E. Thayer is of interest in this connection:

I am absolutely positive that mallards, black ducks, gadwalls, widgeons, green-winged and blue-winged teal, shovelers, and pintails begin mating at Currituck Sound, North Carolina, by February 15. By the 1st of March they are mated. The law should protect them then, for if one is shot, the other will keep flying about until within easy range. There is not a shadow of doubt that the ducks I have named are mated before they migrate, and if we do not want to exterminate them, laws should protect them from the time they leave the South.

Above have been outlined the causes, past and present, of the great diminution in the numbers of the ducks. The practical problem of to-day is the present and future preservation of the remnant. It goes without saying that all ducks should be protected during the breeding season. Notes in the following pages under the different species show the dates at which the earliest eggs have been found, and from these dates it is easy to determine the beginning of the breeding season. The wood duck, in northern Florida, begins nesting by the middle of February and the black duck, in Massachusetts, by April 20. It follows, therefore, that at the very latest these ducks should not be disturbed in Florida after February nor in Massachusetts after April 1. These dates apply to corresponding latitudes in the Mississippi Valley, and the 1st of May would be the latest date for Minnesota and North Dakota. On the Pacific slope the corresponding nesting dates are from late March in southern California to late April in the State of Washington.

Protection during the breeding season is the least that any friend of the ducks would advise. The present rapid diminution in the number of waterfowl can not be stayed, however, by such partial measures. Nothing short of the absolute prohibition of spring shooting in every part of the country should be advocated by those who believe that duck shooting should be enjoyed by future generations.

Another phase of protection relates to the proper regulation of shooting during the fall and winter. This phase concerns a much larger number of species of waterfowl than the question of hunting during the breeding season. For although only 24 species nest within the United States, 46 species are found here during winter, as will appear from the following lists:

WINTER RANGES.

SPECIES THAT WINTER PRINCIPALLY IN THE UNITED STATES AND SOUTHWARD.

Hooded merganser,[a] *Lophodytes cucullatus.*

Mallard, *Anas boschas* (on the Pacific coast to the Aleutian Islands).

Black duck, *Anas obscura.*

Red-legged duck, *Anas obscura rubripes* (occasional in winter in Nova Scotia).

Florida duck, *Anas fulvigula.*

Spotted black duck, *Anas fulvigula maculosa.*

Gadwall, *Chaulelasmus streperus.*

Baldpate,[a] *Mareca americana.*

Green-winged teal, *Nettion carolinense.*

Blue-winged teal,[a] *Querquedula discors.*

Shoveler,[a] *Spatula clypeata.*

Pintail,[a] *Dafila acuta.*

Wood duck,[a] *Aix sponsa.*

Redhead,[a] *Aythya americana.*

Canvasback,[a] *Aythya vallisneria.*

Scaup duck, *Aythya marila* (rare in southern Canada and on the Pacific coast to the Aleutians).

Lesser scaup duck,[a] *Aythya affinis.*

Ring-necked duck,[a] *Aythya collaris.*

American golden-eye, *Clangula clangula americana* (rare in southern Canada, and on the Pacific coast to the Aleutians).

Buffle-head, *Charitonetta albeola* (on the Pacific coast to the Aleutians).

Ruddy duck,[a] *Erismatura jamaicensis.*

Lesser snow goose,[a] *Chen hyperborea.*

Greater snow goose, *Chen hyperborea nivalis.*

Blue goose, *Chen cærulescens.*

Ross goose, *Chen rossii.*

American white-fronted goose, *Anser albifrons gambeli.*

Canada goose,[a] *Branta canadensis.*

Hutchins goose,[a] *Branta canadensis hutchinsii.*

White-cheeked goose, *Branta canadensis occidentalis.*

Cackling goose,[a] *Branta canadensis minima.*

Brant, *Branta bernicla glaucogastra.*

Black brant, *Branta nigricans.*

Fulvous tree-duck, *Dendrocygna fulva.*

Whistling swan,[a] *Olor columbianus.*

Trumpeter swan,[a] *Olor buccinator.*

SPECIES THAT WINTER IN THE UNITED STATES AND CANADA.

American merganser, *Merganser americanus.*

Red-breasted merganser, *Merganser serrator.*

Barrow golden-eye, *Clangula islandica.*

Old squaw, *Harelda hyemalis.*

Harlequin duck, *Histrionicus histrionicus.*

American eider, *Somateria dresseri.*

Spectacled eider, *Somateria spectabilis.*

American scoter, *Oidemia americana.*

White-winged scoter, *Oidemia deglandi.*

Surf scoter, *Oidemia perspicillata.*

If ducks are to be protected for reasons other than esthetic, there must be an open season. Most will agree that so far as the perpetuation of species alone is concerned this open season should be during migration, and preferably during the fall migration. The data presented later in this bulletin show that ducks begin to leave their

---

[a] Winters also in southern British Columbia.

breeding grounds late in August, but that active migration does not occur until September. A shooting season in northern New England or the northern portion of the Mississippi Valley that began September 1 would satisfy the demands of conservative sportsmen of these sections. In the southern United States, however, this date would anticipate by a full month the time when enough ducks arrive to make hunting worth while, and at Currituck Sound, North Carolina, shooting does not begin until November.

In the northern half of the United States the great body of ducks and geese depart with the advent of freezing weather, and but few linger after early November. On the other hand, south of the Ohio River and Chesapeake Bay the ducks and geese remain all winter, and, unless protected, will be harassed throughout the entire cold season. The greatest slaughter of ducks now occurs in the section named, especially in the Mississippi Valley from southern Missouri southward, and here more stringent laws are needed. It is claimed above that the shooting season should be confined to the period of migration, and if this is true then it follows that fall shooting should cease as soon as, or soon after, fall migration has ceased. Regular migration has closed by the first of December, and though the birds are constantly shifting their position all through the winter as the weather changes, these movements can hardly be called migration.

MIGRATION.

Ducks, geese, and swans are migratory. While many breed under the torrid sun of the Tropics, others migrate to the most distant parts of the world for the purpose of nesting. As far into the frozen north as land extends geese summer and successfully rear their young.

A few species are nonmigratory, and individuals of other species, as the ruddy duck, remain through the year near the nesting grounds; but most of the ducks and geese are strictly migratory and some perform extensive journeys. The brant of northern Greenland, for instance, probably spend the winter along the South Atlantic coast of the United States. Some of the blue-winged teal that nest in southern Canada desert North America in fall and cross the equator to spend the winter in central South America. Some of the pintail ducks of Alaska and northeastern Asia cross the equator to the islands of the South Pacific, 4,000 miles from their breeding grounds.

Most waterfowl, in migrating, follow the same route both in spring and fall. The ducks that migrate north along the Mississippi River in spring probably are the same individuals that traversed this route the previous autumn. Among the geese there is a single exception to this rule. The common eastern brant (*Branta bernicla glaucogastra*) in spring passes north along the Atlantic coast to the Gulf of Saint

Lawrence, thence almost due north for 2,000 miles to its breeding grounds, but it is practically unknown in the interior of Canada. In the fall many thousands migrate along the west shore of Hudson Bay and from its southern borders cross to the Atlantic coast. Thus the migration route is in the form of an ellipse some 3,000 miles long north and south by 1,000 miles wide.

Probably in no other region in the world do so large a proportion of the birds migrate approximately north and south as in North America north of the Gulf of Mexico. The outlines of the coast, the courses of the large rivers, and the trend of the mountain chains unite to make northward and southward migration easy and natural. In the case of ducks, however, there is a factor that causes thousands of individuals of several species to take a northwest-and-southeast route. The Atlantic coast from Chesapeake Bay to South Carolina is especially favorable as a winter home for ducks and until recent years countless flocks swarmed throughout this district. Such other birds as winter in this region breed principally in New England and northward along the Atlantic slope to Labrador. But northeastern North America east of Hudson Bay harbors only a small number of ducks in summer. They prefer the marshes, lakes, and streams of the districts west of Hudson Bay, and the great bulk of North American ducks breed there. Thus there are two great districts, one suitable for a summer home and the other for winter, and the migration route between them is nearly northwest and southeast, between Chesapeake Bay and Great Slave Lake. Through much of the intervening 2,000 miles is a succession of lakes, large and small, that find no counterpart elsewhere on this hemisphere, and which furnish ideal conditions for ducks, both as regards food and shelter.

Among the most conspicuous species that follow this migration route are the redhead, canvasback, and greater scaup. Less abundant, though still numerous, are the baldpate, pintail, and lesser scaup, while the route is extensively used also by the mallard, gadwall, shoveler, and ring-necked duck. Nearly all the individuals of these 10 species that winter along the Atlantic coast reach their winter home by a pronounced southeastward migration, though it must be understood that these individuals constitute only a small percentage of the vast army of these same species that breed in central Canada.

One of the principal winter homes of North American ducks and geese is the State of California, where congregates during this season the larger part of all the individuals that breed west of the Rocky Mountains.

DISTRIBUTION.

The family of ducks, geese, and swans is represented in North America by 63 species and 8 subspecies—a total of 71 recognized forms; but the following 7 of these do not range so far north as the United States:

Muscovy duck, *Cairina moschata.*
Diaz duck, *Anas diazi.*
Abert duck, *Anas aberti.*
Bahama duck, *Pœcilonetta bahamensis.*
White-faced tree-duck, *Dendrocygna viduata.*

Whistling duck, *Dendrocygna arborea.*
Southern red-billed tree-duck, *Dendrocygna discolor.*

There remain 64 species and subspecies that occur in the United States and northward, but 11 of these are only accidental in North America. One of them, *Mareca penelope,* has been recorded about 80 times in various parts of the United States, Canada, and Greenland. *Nettion crecca* has been captured about twenty times in the same regions. *Netta rufina* has been found only once—in New York market. The other 7 occur more or less regularly in Greenland, but are not known on the mainland of North America. These 11 species are:

European smew, *Mergus albellus.*
Widgeon,[a] *Mareca penelope.*
European teal,[a] *Nettion crecca.*
Ruddy sheldrake, *Casarca casarca.*
Rufous-crested duck, *Netta rufina.*
Velvet scoter, *Oidemia fusca.*

White-fronted goose, *Anser albifrons.*
Bean goose, *Anser fabalis.*
Brant, *Branta bernicla.*
Barnacle goose, *Branta leucopsis.*
Whooping swan, *Olor cygnus.*

Four species of eider ducks and the emperor goose are so decidedly boreal that they do not come south to the United States even in winter. These are:

Steller eider, *Polysticta stelleri.*
Spectacled eider, *Arctonetta fischeri.*
Northern eider, *Somateria mollissima borealis* (rare on the New England coast).

Pacific eider, *Somateria v-nigra.*
Emperor goose, *Philacte canagica.* (Accidental in California.)

Deducting these, there are 54 species which regularly visit the United States during some portion of the year. Many of these, however, spend the breeding season north of the United States, and come south only in the winter season. Among these last are included both species of swans and most of the geese. Several species of ducks select Canada as their principal breeding ground, but a few individuals remain to breed in the northern part of the United States or in the mountains of the West. These are the scaup (*Aythya marila*), American golden-eye (*Clangula clangula americana*), Barrow golden-eye (*Clangula islandica*), buffle-head (*Charitonetta albeola*), harlequin

---

[a] Occurs in the United States; *Netta rufina* but once.

duck (*Histrionicus histrionicus*), American eider (*Somateria dresseri*), and white-winged scoter (*Oidemia deglandi*). But the individuals which breed in the United States are so few—in the case of *Somateria dresseri* less than a dozen pairs—that they may be ignored in this discussion. Five other species of ducks breed entirely north of the United States, making, in all, 29 species that remain in summer north of our boundaries, as follows:

SPECIES THAT BREED CHIEFLY NORTH OF THE UNITED STATES.

Red-breasted merganser, *Merganser serrator* (rare in the northern United States).

Red-legged duck, *Anas obscura rubripes.*

Scaup, *Aythya marila* (rare in the northern United States).

American golden-eye, *Clangula clangula americana* (rare in the northern United States).

Barrow golden-eye, *Clangula islandica* (rare in the Rocky Mountains of the United States).

Buffle-head, *Charitonetta albeola* (rare in the northern United States).

Old-squaw, *Harelda hyemalis.*

Harlequin duck, *Histrionicus histrionicus* (rare in the mountains of the northwestern United States).

American eider, *Somateria dresseri* (rare in Maine).

King eider, *Somateria spectabilis.*

American scoter, *Oidemia americana.*

White-winged scoter, *Oidemia deglandi* (rare in North Dakota).

Surf scoter, *Oidemia perspicillata.*

Lesser snow goose, *Chen hyperborea.*

Greater snow goose, *Chen hyperborea nivalis.*

Blue goose, *Chen cærulescens.*

Ross goose, *Chen rossii.*

White-fronted goose, *Anser albifrons gambeli.*

Hutchins goose, *Branta canadensis hutchinsii.*

Cackling goose, *Branta canadensis minima.*

White-bellied brant, *Branta bernicla glaucogastra.*

Black brant, *Branta nigricans.*

Whistling swan, *Olor columbianus.*

Trumpeter swan, *Olor buccinator* (formerly a few in the northern United States).

SPECIES THAT BREED CHIEFLY NORTH OF THE ARCTIC CIRCLE, WITH THE NORTHERNMOST LATITUDE AT WHICH THE SPECIES HAS BEEN OBSERVED IN THE WESTERN HEMISPHERE.

Old-squaw, *Harelda hyemalis*, 82°.

Steiler eider, *Polysticta stelleri*, 71°.

Spectacled eider, *Arctonetta fischeri*, 71°.

Northern eider, *Somateria mollissima borealis*, 82°.

Pacific eider, *Somateria v-nigra*, 76°.

King eider, *Somateria spectabilis*, 82°.

Lesser snow goose, *Chen hyperborea*, 74°.

Greater snow goose, *Chen hyperborea nivalis*, 72° (accidental at 82°).

Ross snow goose, *Chen rossii*, 68°.

American white-fronted goose, *Anser albifrons gambeli*, 71°.

Hutchins goose, *Branta canadensis hutchinsii*, 70°.

Cackling goose, *Branta canadensis minima*, 71°.

White-bellied brant, *Branta bernicla glaucogastra*, 82°.

Black brant, *Branta nigricans*, 76°.

Whistling swan, *Olor columbianus*, 74°.

SOUTHERN SPECIES, WITH NORTHERN LIMIT OF BREEDING RANGE.

Florida duck, *Anas fulvigula* (northern Florida).

Mottled duck, *Anas fulvigula maculosa* (northern Texas; accidental in Kansas).

Masked duck, *Nomonyx dominicus* (southern Texas).

Black-bellied tree-duck, *Dendrocygna autumnalis* (southern Texas).

Fulvous tree-duck, *Dendrocygna fulva* (central California).

WESTERN SPECIES, WITH EASTERN LIMIT OF REGULAR RANGE.

Cinnamon teal, *Querquedula cyanoptera* (Kansas).

Steller eider, *Polysticta stelleri* (Alaska).

Spectacled eider, *Arctonetta fischeri* (Alaska).

Pacific eider, *Somateria v-nigra* (Mackenzie).

Ross goose, *Chen rossii* (Hudson Bay).

White-cheeked goose, *Branta canadensis occidentalis* (Nevada).

Cackling goose, *Branta canadensis minima* (California).

Black brant, *Branta nigricans* (Nevada and Mackenzie).

Emperor goose, *Philacte canagica* (Alaska).

SOUTHERN LIMITS OF SPECIES WHOSE WINTER RANGE EXTENDS SOUTH OF THE UNITED STATES.

American merganser, *Merganser americanus* (Mexico, accidental).

Red-breasted merganser, *Merganser serrator* (Mexico).

Hooded merganser, *Lophodytes cucullatus* (Mexico).

Mallard, *Anas boschas* (Panama).

Black duck, *Anas obscura* (Jamaica, accidental).

Gadwall, *Chaulelasmus streperus* (Mexico).

Baldpate, *Mareca americana* (Costa Rica).

Green-winged teal, *Nettion carolinense* (Honduras).

Blue-winged teal, *Querquedula discors* (Chile).

Cinnamon teal, *Querquedula cyanoptera* (Patagonia).

Shoveler, *Spatula clypeata* (Colombia).

Pintail, *Dafila acuta* (Panama).

Wood duck, *Aix sponsa* (Mexico).

Redhead, *Aythya americana* (Mexico).

Canvasback, *Aythya vallisneria* (Guatemala, accidental).

Scaup duck, *Aythya marila* (Bahamas).

Lesser scaup duck, *Aythya affinis* (Panama).

Ring-necked duck, *Aythya collaris* (Guatemala).

American golden-eye, *Clangula clangula americana* (Mexico).

Buffle-head, *Charitonetta albeola* (Mexico).

White-winged scoter, *Oidemia deglandi* (Mexico).

Surf scoter, *Oidemia perspicillata* (Mexico).

Ruddy duck, *Erismatura jamaicensis* (Costa Rica, accidental).

Masked duck, *Nomonyx dominicus* (Argentina).

Lesser snow goose, *Chen hyperborea* (Mexico).

American white-fronted goose, *Anser albifrons gambeli* (Mexico).

Hutchins goose, *Branta canadensis hutchinsii* (Mexico).

White-cheeked goose, *Branta canadensis occidentalis* (Mexico).

Black brant, *Branta nigricans* (Mexico).

Black-bellied tree-duck, *Dendrocygna autumnalis* (Panama).

Fulvous tree-duck, *Dendrocygna fulva* (Argentina).

Whistling swan, *Olor columbianus* (Mexico).

SUMMARY.

Species breeding regularly in the northern United States................... 19

Southern species ranging north to the southern United States............... 5

Species breeding in the United States....................................... 24

Species wintering in the United States but breeding northward.............. 24

Species breeding or wintering in the United States......................... 48

Species breeding and wintering north of the United States................. 5

Species breeding chiefly north of the Arctic Circle....................... 15

Species breeding in the United States and northward....................... 53

European species straggling to North America............................. 11

Species occurring in the United States and northward..................... 64

Southern species not ranging north to the United States.................. 7

Total species and subspecies in North America........................... 71

The material for determining the geographic range of the water-fowl included in this bulletin has been derived from various publications, from museum specimens, and from the notes of field agents of the Biological Survey. The data on migration are derived almost entirely from the migration schedules contributed since 1884 to this Bureau by hundreds of observers distributed throughout the United States and Canada. Opportunity is here taken to extend acknowledgments to the many whose painstaking observations for a long series of years have made possible the present publication.

DISTRIBUTION AND MIGRATION OF DUCKS.

Merganser americanus (Cass.). American Merganser.

Breeding range.—The principal breeding ground of this merganser is in southern Canada from the maritime provinces to Saskatchewan. Southward the species nests quite commonly in Maine, the colder portions of New Hampshire, and in Vermont; it probably has bred casually or accidentally in Massachusetts. It is rather common in the Adirondacks and is not rare in the lake region of northwestern New York. It formerly bred in several of the mountainous counties of central Pennsylvania (Perry, Lancaster, Clinton, and Lycoming), and may yet breed occasionally in that State and in Ohio. It breeds commonly at Ottawa and the Muskoka region in Ontario and it is not rare in the southern part of the Province and on the shores and islands of Lake Ontario. It is common in northern Michigan—rarely as far south as central Michigan—also in southwestern Minnesota (Heron Lake), South Dakota (Fort Sisseton, Black Hills), and south in the Rocky Mountains to northern New Mexico (near Santa Fe), north central Arizona (Fort Verde), and the Sierras of California.

The breeding range extends north to central Ungava (Hamilton River), Hudson Bay (York Factory), Great Slave Lake, and on the Pacific coast regularly to the Queen Charlotte Islands, and rarely to the base of the Alaskan Peninsula at about latitude 60° (Iak Lake, July 24, 1896).

Winter range.—On the Atlantic coast this duck ranges from Maine to South Carolina, rarely to Georgia and Florida; in mild winters it occurs as far north as Prince Edward Island; in the interior it winters from the Gulf of Mexico to southern Ontario, Lake Michigan, Kansas, northern Colorado, Idaho, British Columbia, and rarely to Unalaska Island and the Pribilof Islands. In winter it reaches northern Mexico and northern Lower California. It occurs occasionally in the Bermudas.

Spring migration.—Though the northward movement of this merganser begins early—late February—and there is much activity in the Mississippi Valley in March, on the Atlantic coast the advance beyond the usual winter home is comparatively late. The average date of arrival at Montreal is April 5; Ottawa, Ontario, April 16; Prince Edward Island, April 21. The first merganser was seen on Hamilton River, Ungava, May 28. At Heron Lake, Minnesota, the average date of arrival is March 26 (earliest March 17, 1886); average at Aweme, Manitoba, April 11. The larger number have left the winter range by early April; but along the middle Atlantic coast a few are seen in May, while on the Massachusetts coast nonbreeders occur all summer.

Eggs have been taken at Kingston, Ontario, April 10, 1902; at Godbout, Quebec, May 12, 1884; on Hamilton River, Ungava, June 25; eggs incubated one week, on Lake Tagish, Yukon, June 30, 1899; young in northern California May 21.

Fall migration.—A few of this species start south in August (Woods Hole, Mass., August 26, 1890), but in general the American merganser is a late migrant, passing south only when forced by winter storms. The average date of arrival on the Massachusetts coast is October 5, and on Chesapeake Bay October 15. The average date when the last are seen on Prince Edward Island is November 1; Montreal, November 6; Ottawa, Ontario, November 21.

Merganser serrator (Linn.). Red-breasted Merganser.

Breeding range.—Most of the summer home of this species in the Western Hemisphere lies north of the United States, though a few nest in Maine (Houlton, Magalloway River, Isle au Haute), and farther south on Sable Island, Nova Scotia; also in northern New York (Adirondacks), Michigan, Wisconsin (Green Bay), Minnesota (St. Paul), and probably in Oregon (Crooked River and Camp Harney). The breeding range extends far north to Greenland (Scoresby Sound, Upernavik), Cumberland Gulf, Mackenzie (Fort Anderson), Alaska (Icy Cape), and the northern coast of Siberia. The species breeds commonly on the whole western coast of Alaska, the Near Islands, the Yukon Basin, and south to southern British Columbia. It breeds commonly also in northern Europe and northern Asia, whence it retires in winter to southern Europe and central Asia.

Winter range.—A single specimen was taken near Habana, Cuba, in December, 1891, and this seems to be the only record south of the eastern United States. The species is not rare in winter in Florida and along the Gulf coast to Texas; thence it is quite rare in New Mexico and Arizona, but is common throughout the whole of California and south to Lower California (La Paz). It is common in winter on the Atlantic coast as far as Maine, and remains around the Gulf of Saint Lawrence until the bays freeze. It is not uncommon even in Greenland during the winter. In the interior it braves the winter on the Great Lakes and north to Wisconsin, Nebraska, Colorado, and Utah; north on the Pacific coast to southern British Columbia; it is casual on the Hawaiian Islands and the Bermudas.

Spring migration.--The red-breasted merganser winters so far north that few migration data are available. The species is most common on the Massachusetts coast during the first half of April, though migrants begin to pass a month earlier. The average date of arrival at Montreal is April 16 (earliest, April 6, 1894); at North River, Prince Edward Island, April 21 (earliest, April 15, 1891); Lake Mistassini, Ungava, May 11, 1895; Heron Lake, Minn., April 2, 1884, April 4, 1885; Aweme, Manitoba, April 22, 1899; Fort Keogh, Mont., April 27, 1889; Chilcat, Alaska, May 8, 1882; mouth of the Yukon about the middle of May; Kowak River, Alaska, middle of June (1899). The region in the United States to the south of the breeding ground is deserted in May, except by a few cripples and nonbreeders, some of which are present all summer on the coasts of New Jersey and New England.

Fall migration.—The first arrival in 1896 at Monterey, Cal., was noted October 9; about the same time the species appears in the corresponding latitude on the Atlantic coast. Indeed, October can be said to be the month of arrival in the winter home, and of departure from the most northern breeding grounds; the last was seen on the Mackenzie River, about latitude 63°, October 15 and 16, 1903.

Lophodytes cucullatus (Linn.). Hooded Merganser.

Breeding range.—This merganser breeds locally throughout much of North America, from Florida (Fort Myers and Titusville), Georgia, South Carolina, Tennessee, Kansas, Colorado, northern New Mexico, Nevada, and Oregon, north to Newfoundland, southern Labrador, Hudson Bay (Fort Churchill, latitude 62°), Great Slave Lake, and central British Columbia (Cariboo district). One specimen was seen at Fort Wrigley, Mackenzie River, latitude 63°, where possibly it may breed; it is accidental in Alaska (St. Michael, October, 1865), Bermudas, Europe. In the Southern States mentioned the species is quite rare and local, and the same seems to be true of all the district north of Maine and east of Ontario. The species is most common from latitude 44° to latitude 60°, between the Rocky Mountains and Lake Huron.

Winter range.—It remains during the winter rarely as far north as Massachusetts, Pennsylvania, Lake Michigan, Nebraska, Colorado, Utah, and southern British Columbia. It is more common in the central districts and Gulf States. A few migrate to Cuba, Central Mexico (Orizaba, City of Mexico), and southern Lower California.

Spring migration.—Since the hooded merganser breeds over much of its winter range, it is difficult to determine when its spring migration begins. Migratory movements occur in late February, and average dates of arrival are: Western New York, March; Montreal, early April; Ottawa, Ontario, April 18 (earliest, March 21, 1903); southern Michigan, March 19; central Iowa, March 22 (earliest, March 5, 1895);

Heron Lake, Minn., April 5 (earliest, March 20, 1889). On March 28, 1877, young, a week old, were found in central Florida. Eggs have been taken on April 20 in Illinois and on April 29 in southern Ontario.

Fall migration.—The species arrives in the valley of Mexico in October and in southern California in November. Many years' observations at Alexandria, Va., fix the average date of arrival there as October 26, and November 22 as the average date when the hooded merganser becomes common. The average date when the last left Montreal was October 29; southern Minnesota, November 10, and central Iowa, November 22.

Mergus albellus Linn. Smew.

This is an Old World duck which has been taken once as an accidental visitor to North America. The basis for its inclusion in the list is a single specimen, an adult female, now in the British Museum, which was purchased from the Hudson Bay Company (Cat. Birds Brit. Mus., XXVII, p. 468, 1895). There is no evidence as to the locality of its capture.

Anas boschas Linn. Mallard.

Breeding range.—The northern half of the United States west of Pennsylvania, and the whole of Canada west of Hudson Bay, constitute the principal breeding range in the Western Hemisphere of the mallard—the commonest duck on the North American continent and probably in the world. In eastern North America the place of the mallard is taken by the black duck, and the former is rather rare, though a few breed in eastern Ontario about Lake Erie, locally in western New York, and south to Maryland. Though unknown as a breeder on the mainland east of Hudson Bay, the mallard is rather common in Greenland, breeding north to Godthaab and Angmagsalik and wandering to Upernavik. Throughout New England and the Maritime Provinces it is a rare migrant, and while some of the records of its breeding in these districts may be correct, it is no more than a casual summer resident.

In the interior the breeding range extends regularly south to latitude 41° and a few breed south to southern Indiana, southern Illinois, central Missouri, and southern Kansas. The breeding range bends south in the Rocky Mountains to southern New Mexico and on the Pacific coast to Lower California (San Pedro Martir Mountains).

The breeding range extends north to Fort Churchill, to the Arctic coast in the Mackenzie Valley, and to Kotzebue Sound and the Fur Seal Islands in Alaska.

The mallard is one of the earliest birds to breed. The nesting season extends from early April in southern California and the first week of May in northern Indiana, to early June in the Mackenzie Valley and the Yukon Delta, and the last week of June in Greenland.

It is one of the common ducks of the Old World, breeding in the Northern Hemisphere and ranging south in winter to central Africa and southern Asia.

Winter range.—The mallard is a fresh-water duck, and in general it winters as far north as open fresh water is found. The greater number spend the winter in the southern half of the Mississippi Valley, and for many years this was the source of a large part of the market supply. The numbers killed were almost incredible. Big Lake, Arkansas, was and still is one of the favorite resorts, and during the winter of 1893–94 a single gunner sold 8,000 mallards, while the total number sent to market from this one place amounted to 120,000. Fortunately both Arkansas and Missouri now forbid market shooting, and this deplorable slaughter has been decidedly lessened.

This species winters casually in eastern Massachusetts and central New York, accidentally in Nova Scotia, and regularly from Virginia to northern Florida. It is less common in central Florida, and has been recorded in the Bermudas, Bahamas, Cuba, Jamaica, Grenada, Carriacou, Panama, and Costa Rica. Most of these localities have only one record each, showing that the mallard is only a straggler to the southeast of the United States. There seems to be no record for Central America from Costa Rica to Mexico. The species is a common winter resident of northern Mexico and ranges south to Jalapa, the Valley of Mexico, Colima, and southern Lower California.

The northern winter limit in the interior is in Ohio, northern Indiana, southern Wisconsin, Nebraska, Wyoming, and central Montana. The species is common in winter along the whole Pacific coast as far north as the Aleutian Islands.

Spring migration.—It is among the earliest of ducks to move northward and forms a large proportion of the early flocks. The portion of the central Mississippi Valley that forms the extreme winter range is invaded by the spring migrants the latter part of February; Frankfort, Ind. (average for ten years), February 21; central Illinois (twelve years), February 22; central Missouri (sixteen years), February 26; Keokuk, Iowa (nine years), February 24; southern Kansas (eleven years), February 18; southeastern Nebraska (five years), February 19. Just north of the winter range average dates of spring arrival are: Erie, Pa., March 5; central New York, March 23; Oberlin, Ohio, March 21; southern Michigan, March 9; southern Ontario, March 24; Ottawa, Ontario, March 27; Chicago, Ill. (eleven years), March 19; southern Wisconsin (twelve years), March 21; Spirit Lake, Iowa, March 10; Heron Lake, Minn., March 11; central South Dakota (fourteen years), March 16; Larimore, N. Dak. (twelve years), March 28; Terry, Mont., March 26. The mallard crosses into central Canada early in April, and the average date of arrival at Aweme, Manitoba (ten years), is April 3 (earliest March 24, 1905); Qu' Appelle, Saskatchewan (six years), April 10 (earliest, March 26, 1905). The earliest migrants were seen at Fort Resolution May 7, 1860; near Fort Providence, April 27, 1904; Fort Simpson, May 3, 1904; Kowak River, Alaska, May 17, 1899.

The last one seen in 1892 at Shellmound, Miss., was on April 5; in northern Texas one was seen as late as May 6, 1889. In central Missouri, where a few remain to breed, the average date when the last migrants are seen is March 28.

Fall migration.—In the fall this species returns with the general mass of ducks, and the average date of its arrival at Alexandria, Va., is September 21 (earliest, August 28, 1896); it becomes common October 27; at Chicago, Ill., September 27; Grinnell, Iowa, September 17; and in northern Texas October 11. The first one was noted at San Angelo, Tex., August 10, 1883, and at Austin, Tex., September 1, 1893.

The mallard is one of the moderately hardy ducks, and remains in the north until the lakes begin to freeze. Average dates when the last were seen are: Montreal, Canada, October 26 (latest, November 13, 1897); Scotch Lake, New Brunswick, November 7; Ottawa, Ontario (nine years), November 5 (latest, November 14, 1904); Aweme, Manitoba (eight years), November 12 (latest, November 23, 1902); Chicago, Ill., November 13; English Lake, Ind., December 9; southern Minnesota (ten years), November 22 (latest, December 11, 1890); central Iowa (12 years), November 15 (latest, November 27, 1903); central Nebraska, November 18 (latest, November 26, 1899).

Anas obscura Gmel.   Black Duck.

Breeding range.—The group of 'black' or 'dusky' ducks comprises several species which closely resemble each other and which have been distinguished only in recent years. The black duck is the common breeding duck of New England and northern New York, south of which it breeds not rarely on Long Island and locally in Pennsylvania (Bradford County), New Jersey (Long Beach), Delaware, and Maryland (Ocean City, Barrow Springs). To the westward the breeding range extends south to Ohio (formerly), Indiana (Lake County), Illinois, Iowa (Spirit Lake), and Minnesota (Kandiyohi County). It breeds rarely and locally over much of Wisconsin, but breeds more commonly in Michigan and southern Ontario. It is a very common summer resident of Quebec, New Brunswick, Nova Scotia, and the islands of the Gulf of St. Lawrence. The most northern points at which it breeds are in southern Labrador and Newfoundland. Somewhere in Labrador and in northern Ontario this form meets the more northern form, the red-legged duck (*Anas obscura rubripes*), but the dividing line between the two is unknown. A specimen from the Straits of Belle Isle is *obscura;* one from Okak, Labrador, is intermediate, and one from Ungava Bay, only a few miles farther north, is *rubripes.*

The black duck breeds so early that young have been found at Old Saybrook, Conn., May 5, and eggs at Rehoboth, Mass., April 30.

Winter range.—This species is accidental in winter in the West Indies (Jamaica), rare in the Bermudas, and rare in central Florida (Gainesville) and also in Alabama. From Georgia northward it is more common, and from North Carolina to New Jersey it is one of the abundant winter ducks. Black ducks, including both *A. obscura* and *A. rubripes,* are abundant at this season around Long Island and on the shores of Rhode Island and Massachusetts, but although a few *A. obscura* winter in Massachusetts, the greater number are *A. rubripes.* West of the Alleghenies there is uncertainty as to which form preponderates in winter. *A. obscura* is a tolerably common winter resident of Louisiana, but *A. rubripes* reaches Arkansas, and one form or the other winters as far north as southern Ohio, southern Indiana, and southern Illinois. In migration *A. obscura* is rare west to eastern Nebraska (Fairmont, Gresham, Calhoun) and eastern Kansas (Reno County, Wichita, and Lawrence). Notes on the migration of this species are for the most part included under those of *A. rubripes.*

Anas obscura rubripes Brewst. Red-legged Black Duck.

Breeding range.—As stated under the last species, a breeding duck from Okak, northeastern Labrador, is considered intermediate between this form and *A. obscura,* while the bird breeding at Ungava Bay is *A. rubripes.* This Ungava Bay record seems to mark the northeastern limit of the species so far as reported. Thence the species extends west to Hudson Bay, as far north at least as Fort Churchill, and is rare or accidental west to Manitoba (Long Lake; Lake Manitoba, October 28, 1900; Delta, September 4, 1902, September, 1903; St. Marks, two, October, 1902), and to Fort Anderson. The southern limit of the breeding range in Ontario has not yet been determined.

Winter range.—Most of the black ducks that winter in Massachusetts are *A. rubripes,* and this is about as far north as the species commonly winters. Along the coast some have been known in winter as far north as Nova Scotia. How far south the species goes has not yet been determined, but it is common on the coast of South Carolina from November to March, and a specimen was taken in Mississippi County, Ark., November 5, 1887. It occurs west to Nebraska (Greenwood, Lincoln, Calhoun) and undoubtedly wanders to eastern Kansas. The northern winter limit in the interior is probably from northwestern Pennsylvania to southern Wisconsin.

Spring migration.—It is impossible to separate the migration records of *A. obscura* and *A. rubripes.* The following migration notes probably refer for the most part to *A. rubripes*, because that form winters farther north. In March extensive northward movements of black ducks occur, but it is not until early April that the birds pass beyond the usual winter range. The average date of arrival for seventeen years in southern Maine is April 7; the earliest, March 19, 1894; the average date for Montreal is April 14, and March 27, 1889, is the earliest; Quebec, average, April 18 (earliest, April 6, 1896); Godbout, Quebec, average, April 21; Prince Edward Island, April 23 (earliest, April 5, 1898). Farther west the average date of arrival in southern Ontario is April 7 (earliest, March 16, 1901); average at Ottawa, April 14 (earliest, March 21, 1903).

Fall migration.—A black duck was seen at Washington, D. C., August 1, 1887; one at Alexandria, Va., August 14, 1886, and one at Hog Island, Va., August 20, 1886; but these are unusually early records. The average of a long series of excellent records at Alexandria, Va., is September 30 for the arrival of the first and October 31 as the average date when they become common. About the middle of October, on the New England coast, they become common enough to usher in the shooting season. These dates, of course, apply to *A. obscura.* There are no exact records of the time when *A. rubripes* arrives from its northern breeding grounds, but it is supposed that it reaches New England about the first week in October. In winter it remains as far north as it can find open water. The average date when the last leave Ottawa, Ontario, is November 7 (latest, November 21, 1892); average at Montreal, November 6 (latest, November 14, 1896). The last one was seen at Prince Edward Island November 13, 1889, and December 8, 1890.

Anas fulvigula Ridgw. Florida Duck.

A nonmigratory species, breeding commonly in the southern half of Florida, and less commonly in the northern portion. It seems to be absent from northeastern Florida, but occurs along the northwestern coast of the State. Nests in late April and in May, but sometimes much earlier, for downy young have been taken as early as April 6.

Anas fulvigula maculosa (Senn.). Mottled Duck.

Resident in Texas and southern Louisiana (Lake Arthur). In Texas it occurs from the mouth of the Rio Grande northward and west to about the middle of the State. It is accidental in Kansas (Neosho Falls, March 11, 1876). It breeds throughout most if not all of its Texas range; the eggs are deposited in April.

[Anas diazi Ridgw. Diaz Black Duck.

A form of 'black duck' closely resembling *Anas fulvigula.* It is nonmigratory and occurs in central Mexico from Chihuahua City to Tepic, Jalisco, Michoacan, the Valley of Mexico, Puebla, and Tlaxcala.]

[**Anas aberti** Ridgw. Albert Duck.

A species known only from the type specimen taken at Mazatlan, Mexico.]

Chaulelasmus streperus (Linn.). Gadwall.

Breeding range.—A large majority of the North American individ-uals of this species breed in the prairie district extending from Mani-toba to the Rocky Mountains, south to western Minnesota, and from northern South Dakota north to the Saskatchewan.

The species breeds commonly from the Rocky Mountains to the Pacific, south to southern Colorado, Utah, Nevada, and in nearly the whole of California; also probably in the Mogollon Mountains of Arizona. The northern range extends to southern British Columbia, Alberta (rarely or casually to Lesser Slave Lake), and to Fort Churchill on Hudson Bay. There is no authentic record for the Mackenzie Valley, and if the specimen in the British Museum labeled "Bering Straits" really was captured there it was a wanderer, as was also one taken at Unalaska, March 18, 1879.

In the Mississippi Valley the gadwall occasionally breeds in northern Nebraska and rarely in Kansas. Formerly it bred in Wisconsin (Hori-con Marsh and Lake Koshkonong), there is one record for Ontario (St. Clair Flats), and one for Anticosti Island. It is only a straggler to New England and the Maritime Provinces north to Quebec and Newfoundland, and east of the Mississippi is rare north of North Carolina.

The gadwall is a common breeder in Europe and Asia, ranging south in winter far into Africa and to southern Asia.

Winter range.—The principal winter home of the gadwall is in the lower Mississippi Valley, especially Texas, Louisiana, and Arkansas. It rarely winters as far north as Illinois, but is more common to the eastward in North Carolina and Florida; accidental in Cuba (twice), Jamaica, and the Bermudas. The winter range extends to the south-ern end of Lower California, to Mazatlan, and the City of Mexico. In northern Mexico the species is common through the winter, and birds have been found paired in May, the late date indicating that they intended to remain and breed. Thence it extends commonly to Utah and Oregon, rarely to Washington and British Columbia.

Spring migration.—Only a few notes on the migration of this species have been recorded. The average date when the first spring migrants reach southern Iowa is March 18 (earliest March 10, 1896), it thus being one of the earlier ducks in this part of its range. It reached Heron Lake, Minn., April 1 (earliest March 17, 1886); Love-land, Colo., March 6, and Terry, Mont., about April 1. The first migrant was seen at Aweme, Manitoba, April 23, 1898, and at Indian Head, Saskatchewan, April 18, 1892, and April 24, 1904. Eggs have been secured at St. Clair Flats, Ontario, about May 30; in western Minnesota, June 14, 1879; northern North Dakota, June 15, 1901; Manitoba, June 5, 1894; Crane Lake, Saskatchewan, June 9, 1894; Nevada, May 29, 1868, and incubated eggs in Los Angeles County, Cal., April 16.

Fall migration.—The first arrived at the southern end of Lower California September 27, 1887; in northern New Mexico the species was abundant the last days of September, 1904. The average date when the last left central Minnesota was November 14.

Mareca penelope (Linn.).   European Widgeon.

This is an Old World species which has occurred as a straggler on the Atlantic coast in Florida, North Carolina, Virginia, Maryland, Pennsylvania, New Jersey, New York, Massachusetts, Nova Scotia, Newfoundland, and Greenland; in the interior it has been found in Illinois, Indiana, Ohio, Michigan, Wisconsin, and Nebraska; on the Pacific coast in California, British Columbia, and Alaska. It is not known to breed anywhere in the Western Hemisphere.

On the Atlantic coast the dates are almost entirely in the fall and winter, from October 20 (near Halifax, Mass.) to March 25 (Keuka Lake, New York)—there are only three records after February 5—while in the interior its occurrence is as strictly confined to the spring, from March 23 (English Lake, Ind.) to April 18 (Sandusky, Ohio). The records for Greenland fall between September 29 and December 17; the California records are mostly in February, while those of British Columbia are from December 25 to February 9, and the two Alaska dates are October 12 and May 27.

Mareca americana (Gmel.).   Baldpate.   American Widgeon.

Breeding range.—A line drawn from the western shore of Hudson Bay to the western shore of Lake Michigan marks, approximately, the eastern boundary of the breeding range of this species, and in the eastern 200 miles of this district it is decidedly uncommon during the nesting season. There are a few records of the bird's breeding in Indiana (Hogback Lake, English Lake) and in Wisconsin (formerly at Koshkonong and Horicon), but not until Minnesota is reached does this duck breed commonly. West of the Mississippi it breeds abundantly in North Dakota, a few in southern South Dakota, and rarely or casually in Nebraska and Kansas. It is a common breeder in Colorado, Utah, and Nevada (Truckee Valley), and probably breeds rarely in Arizona (Mormon Lake), but as yet the species has not been recorded as nesting in California. The main breeding range is northwestern North America from Oregon and Minnesota north to the Mackenzie Valley and central Alaska. A line from Fort Churchill, Hudson Bay, to Franklin Bay is the approximate northeastern boundary of the range, thence west to Kotzebue Sound. If this line from Franklin Bay to Fort Churchill is continued to Chesapeake Bay, it marks the approximate eastern limits at which the species is common in migration. Northeastward the species is known as a rare migrant, in New England hardly more than a straggler, but it has been recorded as far as Newfoundland, southern Labrador (Natashquan), and northern Ontario (Moose River). The baldpate is rather rare on the coast of Alaska, but is more common in the interior, and is a rare or casual visitor to the Near, Commander, and Bermuda islands.

Winter range.—The baldpate is common on the Chesapeake in winter, but as it is rare directly to the northward at all times of the year, it is evident that the migration is from the northwest. Occasionally birds are found in winter as far north as Rhode Island. The species is common during the winter in the Carolinas, less common in Florida and Cuba, and rare in the Bermudas, the Bahamas, Jamaica, Porto Rico, St. Thomas, and Trinidad. It is recorded from Costa Rica, and is a rather common winter resident of northern Guatemala and much of Mexico north of the Valley of Mexico. The winter home in the Mississippi Valley extends north to Illinois, and in the west to New Mexico, Arizona, Utah (probably), and to southern British Columbia. It is probably most common during the winter along the Pacific coast.

Spring migration.—This begins late in February and by early March the species is north of its winter home. Average dates of arrival are: Western New York, March 23; Erie, Pa., March 24; Oberlin, Ohio, March 17; southern Michigan, March 25; Keokuk, Iowa, March 15; central Nebraska, March 17; Loveland, Colo., March 10. The further advance of the species is somewhat slow. The average time of reaching Heron Lake, Minn., is March 29; southern Manitoba, April 20; Terry, Mont., April 8. The first individual was seen at Indian Head, Saskatchewan, April 24, 1904, and at Osler, Saskatchewan, May 2, 1893. These dates indicate an average speed of 17 miles per day from central Nebraska to Heron Lake, and 18 miles per day thence to southern Manitoba. The average rate from Colorado to Montana is 16 miles per day, and the same rate continued northward would bring the first baldpate to Indian Head and Osler at almost exactly the stated dates. If the birds of the Mississippi Valley pass northwest to the Mackenzie Valley, this rate of migration would bring them to Great Slave Lake about the first week in June, whereas the first arrival at Fort Simpson, Mackenzie, was April 28, 1904; and a female was shot at Fort Resolution May 24, 1860, which contained a fully formed egg. It is evident, then, that the earliest arrivals in the Mackenzie Valley come from the southwest, where, in southern British Columbia, the species winters a thousand miles farther north than on the plains. The baldpate arrives at the mouth of the Yukon in early May, and on the Knik River, Alaska, the first bird was noted May 10, 1901. Most of the few spring records in New England are in April, two in February, but the species is apparently less common in the spring than in the fall. The last migrants usually leave Cuba late in April, though in Guatemala they have been seen as late as May.

Fall migration.—The month of September, especially the latter half, sees the arrival of the first baldpates over most of the district between the breeding grounds and Cuba and Louisiana; but these are only the advance scouts; the main body appears in the northern United States early in October, and reaches the middle Atlantic States about the middle of that month.   Dates of arrival are: Middletown, R. I., September 20, 1889; East Hartford, Conn., September 29, 1888; Beaver, Pa., August 30, 1890. Stragglers have been seen in Massachusetts and in northern Pennsylvania as late as the first week in December, but most leave at least a month earlier. The average date at which the last were seen at Ottawa, Ontario, is October 27, latest November 6, 1890; at Keokuk, Iowa, November 13, latest November 18, 1892. The last was seen at Montreal September 20, 1897; Edmonton, Alberta, November 6, 1896; Kowak River, Alaska, September 20, 1898; St. Michael, Alaska, October 1.

Nettion crecca (Linn.). European Teal.

This is a widely distributed Old World species, accidental in the Western Hemisphere. It has been taken in Greenland, Labrador, Nova Scotia, Maine, Massachusetts, Connecticut, Long Island, near Washington, D. C., California, and Alaska. The dates of capture range through every month of the year, except January, August, and October; those for the United States from November to April.

Nettion carolinense (Gmel.). Green-winged Teal.

Breeding range.—A few probably have bred in the mountains of north central Pennsylvania (Lycoming County), and it has been reported as nesting near Buffalo, N. Y. The regular breeding range extends from New Brunswick, through northeastern Quebec and Newfoundland, to Ungava Bay, Labrador, latitude 58°. It is a common migrant in Ontario, and hence undoubtedly breeds in the northern part. It has been recorded as a rare breeder in southern Ontario (Toronto, Point aux Pins, Oshawa, Gravenhurst). The southern boundary of the breeding range to the westward is found in Illinois (Rockford, Lacon, Fernwood), in Michigan (Neebish Island), Wisconsin (Lake Koshkonong, formerly), Minnesota (Faribault, Heron Lake), Nebraska (Dewey Lake, Badger, Valentine), Colorado (Beloit, San Luis Valley), New Mexico (San Miguel County), Utah (Salt Lake), Nevada (Washoe Lake), Oregon (Fort Klamath). The range extends north to the edge of the Barren Grounds from near Fort Churchill, Hudson Bay, to Fort Anderson, to Kotzebue Sound, and nearly to Point Barrow. It breeds throughout the Aleutian Chain to the Near Islands. It is rare as a breeder everywhere in the United States east of the Rocky Mountains, and the main breeding grounds are in west central Canada from Manitoba to Lake Athabasca. It has wandered a few times to the west coast of Greenland, from Nanortalik to Disco Bay, and was once taken in May on the east coast at Nanusek. The species is accidental in Great Britain, the Bermudas, and Hawaii.

Winter range.—South of the United States it is common in Mexico, at least as far as Jalapa, the City of Mexico, Michoacan, and Jalisco; common also in the Bahamas, and rare in Cuba, Jamaica, and Honduras. It has been recorded on the islands of Carriacou, Grenada, and Tobago, of the Lesser Antilles.

It is one of the most abundant ducks throughout the southwestern United States during winter. It is a hardy duck, and in general remains as far north as it can find open fresh water. Thus it winters in western Montana (Great Falls), central Utah, southern Nebraska, southern Iowa, central Illinois, central Indiana (rarely Lake Michigan), western New York, and Rhode Island. It is accidental in Massachusetts in winter, and one was found at Halifax, Nova Scotia, January 14, 1890. The principal winter home in the Mississippi Valley lies south of 37° latitude.

Spring migration.—The green-winged teal is one of the early migrating 'river ducks,' but not quite so early, by about five days, as the mallard. Along the Atlantic slope it passes north of its winter home in early March, and the average date of its arrival in southern Pennsylvania is March 16; southern Connecticut, April 6; Montreal, Canada, April 27, Prince Edward Island, April 26.

The average date of the first arrivals in central Missouri is February 26; central Illinois, March 7; English Lake, Ind., March 15; Keokuk, Iowa (average for twelve years), March 3; central Iowa (fourteen years), March 11; Heron Lake, Minn. (six years), March 24 (earliest March 6, 1887). In its migration along the eastern border of the Plains the green-winged teal is noted at Onaga, Kans., March 8; northern Nebraska, March 12; central South Dakota, March 20; northern North Dakota, April 6; Aweme, Manitoba, April 16, and southern Saskatchewan, April 19. These dates indicate the rather slow rate of only 18 miles a day. The average of five years' records of arrival at Terry, Mont., is March 23, a date about ten days earlier than that at which the species appears in the same latitude in Minnesota. Its winter home on the Pacific coast extends 1,500 miles farther north than on the Atlantic, and hence it is not surprising that the bird has been seen on the middle Yukon by May 3 and at the mouth of the Yukon by May 10.

South of the breeding range the last green-winged teal was seen at Raleigh, N. C., April 13, 1900; Hester, La., April 6, 1902; northern Texas, April 16, 1886. The average date of disappearance for eight years at Keokuk, Iowa, is April 7, latest, April 30, 1892.

Eggs were taken at Nulato, Alaska, latitude 65°, May 20, and no earlier date seems to be recorded for the regions to the south. Eggs have been found at Edmonton, Alberta, latitude 54°, May 27, and in southern Ontario, latitude 45°, May 22. Downy young were seen in the Devils Lake region of North Dakota June 20.

Fall migration.—An average date for the reappearance of the green-winged teal at Erie, Pa., is September 15 (earliest, September 1, 1894); at Alexandria, Va., September 29 (earliest, September 22); but it is not considered common until early November. Corresponding dates of arrival are: Keokuk, Iowa, September 21; central Kansas, September 12; central Texas, September 22; central California, September 17. The last was noted on Prince Edward Island, November 4, 1890; Montreal, Canada, November 1, 1893; Aweme, Manitoba, October 30, 1896; Kowak River, Alaska, September 3, 1898; St. Michael, Alaska, the first week in October. The average date of the last seen in southern Ontario (thirteen years) is October 28 (latest, November 7, 1890); at Keokuk, Iowa (seven years), November 22 (latest, November 27, 1902).

Querquedula discors (Linn.). Blue-winged Teal.

Breeding range.—The principal summer home of this teal is the interior of North America between the Rocky Mountains and the Great Lakes, from Northern Illinois and central Iowa north to Saskatchewan. The species is not common east of the Allegheny Mountains nor on the Pacific slope. It has been recorded as breeding rarely in Rhode Island (Sakonnet, 1890), Maine (Calais), New Brunswick (Kings County, St. John County), Nova Scotia, Anticosti Island and Newfoundland, Quebec (Montreal, Point de Monts), Ungava (Clearwater Lake, latitude 57°), rare in southern Ontario (Toronto), New York (Utica, Auburn, Buffalo, formerly Long Island, Black Pond, Ulster County). It breeds as far south as northern Ohio (Port Clinton, Sandusky), southern Indiana (Gibson County and Wheatland), southern Illinois (Anna), central Missouri (Kings Lake, Warrensburg, Kansas City), central Kansas (Emporia, Wichita, Medicine Lodge, Fort Hays)—casual or accidental breeding at Fort Reno, Okla., and San Antonio and Spring Lake, Texas—southern Colorado (Fort Garland and La Plata County), New Mexico (Santa Rosa; Black Lake, Colfax County; Chloride), probably in Arizona (Mogollon Mountains), central Utah (Thistle Valley, Fairfield), northern Nevada (Truckee Valley, Washoe Lake), and central Oregon (Burns).

The breeding range extends north to central British Columbia (Lac la Hache, 158-Mile House); but the bird is rare or accidental in Alaska (Cape Romanzoff), Alberta (Edmonton), and on Great Slave Lake. Much remains to be learned in regard to the nesting of the blue-winged teal in the West Indies and Central America. It breeds in Jamaica and in the Lesser Antilles, quite probably also in Honduras and in western Mexico (Mazatlan), near the southern end of Lower California.

The resident teal of Jamaica probably should be separated subspecifically as *Querquedula discors inornata* (Gosse), but the eastern and western boundaries of this form remain to be determined.

Winter range.—Blue-winged teal migrate over a vast extent of territory, and are found in winter throughout northern South America south to Brazil, Ecuador, Peru, and Chile. They occur abundantly in Central America, Mexico, and the West Indies, and are equally common during the winter in the Gulf States and north to North Carolina. In the Mississippi Valley few remain much north of the Gulf, though these few are scattered widely as far as southern Indiana and southern Illinois; a few winter in Arizona, and the small number of Pacific coast birds spend the winter in California and north to southern British Columbia.

North of North Carolina this teal can hardly be called a common winter species, though it is not rare on Chesapeake Bay and winters even as far north as Delaware. This species is one of the least hardy of our ducks, and few individuals remain where there is cold and ice.

Spring migration.—The blue-winged teal is among the latest ducks to migrate. The first was noted at Erie, Pa., March 27, 1898; Templeton, Mass., April 1, 1898; Prince Edward Island, April 20, 1888. In central Iowa, where the hardy ducks appear in February, the blue-winged teal was noted on the average (ten years) March 26 (earliest, March 18, 1899); northern Iowa, April 4, and Heron Lake, Minn., April 9. The records of Heron Lake are quite uniform—April 11, 1885; April 11, 1886; April 10, 1887; April 8, 1888; April 9, 1889; April 7, 1890. These dates indicate less variation in the time of arrival of this species than of any other. The blue-winged teal appears in southeastern Nebraska, March 28; central South Dakota, April 2; central North Dakota, April 12; northwestern Minnesota, April 23; Aweme, Manitoba, April 27.

In southern Texas this teal becomes common in spring about the middle of March; about the first week in April is the height of the shooting season in southern Louisiana. The latest migrants have been noted at Gainesville, Fla., April 29, 1887; Baltimore, Md., May 7, 1890; New Orleans, La., May 21, 1898; San Antonio, Tex., May 14, 1902. Eggs have been taken at Canton, Ill., May 16, 1897. Eggs just hatching were found on the Magdalen Islands, Gulf of St. Lawrence, June 16, 1900, and fresh eggs at Waseca, Minn., June 1; in North Dakota, June 12; and at Reaburn, Manitoba, June 4, 1894.

Fall migration.—The blue-winged teal is one of the earliest ducks to move southward; during the month of August it reappears throughout the northern half of the United States and some especially early birds almost reach the Gulf of Mexico. During a period of fourteen years the average date of arrival at Alexandria, Va., was August 31 (earliest, August 18, 1889); they became common on the average September 23, though in the fall of 1887 they were already numerous September 10. The average date of arrival in central Kansas is September 12, and in southern Mississippi, September 16.

The average date at which the last was seen at Montreal was September 25; latest, September 29, 1888; the last one seen on Prince Edward Island in this same year was October 8; Lewiston, Me., November 7, 1901; Cape May, N. J., December 5, 1884.

The average date for eight years when the last one was seen at Ottawa, Ontario, is October 13 (latest, October 27, 1894); Chicago, Ill., October 18 (latest, October 22, 1904); southern Iowa, October 22 (latest, November 4, 1885); central South Dakota, October 7; eastern Nebraska, November 11; central Missouri, November 6 (latest, November 13, 1902). The last one seen in 1896 at Aweme, Manitoba, was on October 30. During the fall migration the blue-winged teal is fairly common on the Bermudas, but it rarely occurs there in spring.

Querquedula cyanoptera (Vieill.). Cinnamon Teal.

Breeding range.—The breeding range of the cinnamon teal differs essentially from that of almost every other duck in the Western Hemisphere. It consists of a large area north of the equator and a similar district south of the equator, and these two homes are separated by a strip about 2,000 miles wide, in which the species is practically unknown. In North America the breeding range extends north to southern British Columbia (Lac la Hache) and southwestern Alberta; east to eastern Wyoming (Lake Como, Cheyenne), western Kansas (Fort Wallace, Meade County); south to northern Lower California (La Grulla, San Rafael Valley, and possibly San Jose del Cabo), northern Mexico (Chihuahua City), southern New Mexico (Carlsbad), and southwestern Texas (Marathon, Rock Spring).

The cinnamon teal occurs sparingly in migration as far east as Houston, Tex., and Omaha, Nebr. It has been noted as accidental at Oak Lake, Manitoba; Big Stone Lake, Minnesota; Lake Koshkonong, Wisconsin; Licking County Reservoir, Ohio; Seneca River and Seneca Lake, New York; Lake Pontchartrain, Lake Cattawatchie, St. Malo, and Opelousas, Louisiana; Mount Pleasant, S. C.; Lake Iamonia and Key West, Florida.

Throughout this breeding area the eggs are deposited during May and June. About six months later the South American colony breeds. The breeding range includes the pampas of Argentina as far north as Buenos Aires, while in the Andes it extends north to central Peru (Santa Luzia). Southward the species breeds as far as the Falkland Islands and the Straits of Magellan. These South American breeders, of course, are not the same birds which nest in North America, for it is true, without exception, that no bird which breeds north of the equator breeds also in the Southern Hemisphere.

Winter range.—The cinnamon teal of North America retires in winter but little south of its breeding range in Mexico as far as Mazatlan, Guanajuato, and the Laguna de Chapulco, Puebla. It is found at this season as far north as Brownsville, Tex., central New Mexico, southern Arizona, and Tulare Lake, California. South of Mexico the only record is of an accidental occurrence in Costa Rica. There is no reliable record as yet for the West Indies.

During the winter season the cinnamon teal of the Southern Hemisphere has been noted as far south as the mouth of the Senger River, in Patagonia, latitude 44° S., and Chiloe Island, Chile, in nearly the same latitude. The northern range in winter is not determinable with exactness from present data. The species passes north to Rio Grande do Sul, Brazil, and to southern Paraguay. It has been noted at Chorillos and Tungasuca, Peru; near Quito, Ecuador; at Bogota and Santa Marta, Colombia. These Ecuador and Colombia teal may be accidental occurrences; it is significant, at least, that all the specimens from Colombia were taken a half a century ago, and the species has not been noted there by recent collectors.

Spring migration.—The northward movement of the cinnamon teal in the United States begins about the 1st of March, and arrivals have been noted at Ash Meadows, Nevada, March 18, 1891; Grangeville, Idaho, April 11, 1887; Chilliwack, British Columbia, April 24, 1888, and April 22, 1889; Beloit, Colo., March 23, 1892; Colorado Springs, April 9, 1882; Loveland, Colo., April 13, 1890; Lay, Colo., April 20, 1890; Omaha, Nebr., April 10, 1896, and April 12, 1897; Lake Como, Wyoming, about May 5.

Fall migration.—Southward migration occurs chiefly in September, and the northern portion of the breeding grounds from British Columbia to eastern Colorado is deserted about the middle of October.

Migration in South America.—The cinnamon teal of South America is migratory in at least part of its range, for in central Argentina it is abundant during the winter season, April to September, and rare or lacking during the breeding period. The species is migratory also in the southern portion of its range in Chile. In northern Chile and in Peru migration records are wanting. The time and direction of the migration of this species in South America correspond closely with those in the United States, but of course the breeding and wintering seasons are reversed, since they are on opposite sides of the equator.

Thus the cinnamon teal is distributed in two distinct colonies, part of the individuals breeding far north of the equator, and the rest about an equal distance to the south. The northern breeders migrate south after nesting, and the southern breeders migrate north. Whether or not the members of these two groups now represent subspecies, they are so much alike as to indicate a common origin and a former continuous breeding range. Whether isolation was gradual or was effected rapidly it is impossible to say, nor do we know the cause.

Casarca casarca (Linn.).   Ruddy Sheldrake.

This is a European, African, and Asiatic species that has been taken several times in western and northern Greenland.

Spatula clypeata (Linn.).   Shoveler.

Breeding range.—The principal North American summer home of the shoveler is in the prairie region of the interior, from a little south of the Canadian border, north to the Saskatchewan. Throughout this region it is common. To the eastward it is rare. It is scarcely common as far as Hudson Bay; nor is it common east of a line from southeastern Michigan to the mouth of Chesapeake Bay, in which latter region it is found only in migration and in winter. In the maritime provinces of Canada, and even north to Newfoundland, the shoveler has been recorded as a rare or casual visitor; but reliable breeding records from this region seem to be lacking. It is rare as a breeder in southern Michigan, and to the eastward is almost accidental in summer, though it has been known to breed at English Lake, northwestern Indiana, and at Long Point, on the north shore of Lake Erie. The regular breeding range extends south to northern Iowa and southern South Dakota; thence southward it breeds rarely and locally in Nebraska and Kansas, and during the summer of 1905 one of the parties of the Biological Survey found it breeding near East Bernard, about latitude 29° 30′, in southeastern Texas. In the western United States the species breeds commonly from Colorado to northern California, and rarely in New Mexico (Santa Rosa), Arizona (Mogollon Mountains), and southern California (Los Angeles County). On the southern coast of Texas the species is not uncommon all summer, though these summer residents are probably nonbreeders. Mated birds have been found in May in northern Chihuahua, Mexico, and at the southern end of Lower California, and it is not improbable that the species may breed locally in these districts, and even south to Lake Chapala, Jalisco.

The northern limit of the usual breeding range is from the valley of the Saskatchewan to central British Columbia. The species is a rare breeder thence northward to the edge of the Barren Grounds, casually to Fort Anderson and Fort McPherson. It is rather rare in the Yukon region, but has been known to breed at Fort Yukon, Nulato, and along the west coast of Alaska from the mouth of the Kuskokwim River to Kotzebue Sound. The shoveler has a wide range in the Eastern Hemisphere, breeding north about to the Arctic Circle, and retiring in winter to northern Africa and southern Asia.

Winter range.—A few pass south in winter to Colombia, South America (Medellin, Bogota), Panama, Costa Rica, and through the West Indies (Cuba, Jamaica, Porto Rico, St. Thomas, Barbados, and Trinidad). It is rare in Florida, and seems not to have been noted in the

Bahamas. The Carolinas are the only place on the Atlantic coast where the species is common. It is not rare in Maryland, and there are a few winter records for New Jersey. The greater portion of the species winters in the southern Mississippi Valley, north rarely to southern Illinois—accidental January 11, 1892, at Lanesboro, Minn.—and south through Mexico to central Guatemala; indeed many hundreds of thousands are said to winter near Lake Chapala, Jalisco. At this season it is found in New Mexico, Arizona, all of California, and less commonly north on the Pacific coast to southern British Columbia. Numbers winter in the Hawaiian Islands. During flight between the winter and summer home it passes through the northeastern United States, not rarely through Pennsylvania and New York, and formerly it was not rare in Massachusetts; but for the last fifteen years there has been hardly more than a single record a year for the whole of New England.

Spring migration.—Records of the movements of this species are not numerous enough to permit exact statements. Migration begins late in February, but is slight before the middle of March, at which time the species begins to appear north of its winter range. Average dates of arrival are: Central Illinois, March 23; central Iowa, March 23 (average of sixteen years); Heron Lake, Minn., March 26; central Nebraska, March 25; central Colorado, March 12; vicinity of Chicago, Ill., April 16; southeastern Minnesota, April 9; central North Dakota, April 13; southern Manitoba (twelve years), April 21; Terry, Mont., April 13. The first were seen near Edmonton, Alberta, May 1, 1901; Fort Chipewyan, Mackenzie, May 7, 1893; Fort Resolution, Mackenzie, May 18, 1860, and at the mouth of the Yukon River the second week in May. The general time of breeding can be learned from the following dates: Haywards, Cal., eggs April 25, 1901; East Bernard, Tex., downy young May 14, 1905; Fort Snelling, Minn., eggs May 23; North Dakota, incubated eggs June 7; Oak Lake, Manitoba, eggs May 24, 1892.

Fall migration.—An individual seen at Erie, Pa., September 6, 1893, marks about the beginning of fall migration, and soon after this, by the middle of the month, the earliest migrants have reached the mouth of the Mississippi River. The larger portion has departed from the northern United States by the middle of October, and the region just north of the winter range is deserted early in November. South of the United States, at the southern end of Lower California, the first arrivals have been recorded October 18; Guaymas, Mexico, November; Panama, October 16; Cuba, September; Jamaica, November; Trinidad, December.

Dafila acuta (Linn.). Pintail.

Breeding range.—This is a common breeding duck throughout a wide stretch of country from North Dakota to the Arctic Ocean and

Alaska. The western shores of Hudson Bay seem to be the eastern limit of the normal breeding ground in North America. A few birds have been seen in Labrador, north to Ungava Bay, on the west coast of Greenland, north to Upernavik, and also in Newfoundland and the Maritime Provinces. But there are only a few breeding records east of the line from the western side of Hudson Bay to the western shore of Lake Michigan; examples are: St. George Island, James Bay; St. Clair Flats, Ontario, and the north shore of Lake Erie. Breeding abundantly along the northern border of the United States from Lake Superior nearly to the Pacific Ocean, the species decreases in numbers southward until it is rare or casual as a breeder in southern Wisconsin, northern Illinois (Will, Calumet Marsh, Grass Lake); southern Minnesota (Faribault, Waverly, Heron Lake); northern Iowa (Hancock County); southern South Dakota (Vermilion, Scotland, Running Water), and northern Nebraska (Kennedy, Hay Lake); accidental near Kansas City, Mo.; abundant in Montana and rare in Wyoming (Lake Desmet), Colorado (Larimer County), and probably Arizona (Mormon Lake); common in British Columbia, and rare and local through Washington (Mabton) and Oregon (Rock Creek Sink) to southern California (Alamitos). The northern limit of the breeding range extends from the Arctic coast northwest of Hudson Bay west to Alaska and the Siberian coast.

The pintail breeds in the northern portions of the Old World and migrates south in winter to northern Africa and southern Asia. A few have been taken in the Bermudas in the fall and winter.

Winter range.—The pintail is common in winter on the coast of North Carolina, and is not uncommon coastwise as far south as Florida; many spend the winter in Cuba, a few pass to Jamaica, and there is one record of the species in Porto Rico; it is one of the common winter ducks from Mexico to Costa Rica, rare in Panama; a few winter as far north as Pennsylvania and New Jersey, while accidentals in winter have been recorded from Long Island and Lynn, Mass. Only a few winter in the Mississippi Valley north of southern Illinois, and thence the winter home extends through Texas, New Mexico, and Arizona to the Pacific coast, where it is abundant at this season as far north as southern British Columbia. The species winters casually in southern Ohio and southern Indiana, while of late years it has become a regular local winter resident in southern Wisconsin.

Spring migration.—The pintail vies with the mallard in the earliness of its spring movements; these two, with the Canada goose, are among the first of the waterfowl to wing their way northward. Even in February, while winter still holds sway, restless adventurers appear in much of the region, which, except in a few favored spots, forbids residence through the winter. The average date of arrival of these birds in central Indiana (fourteen years) is February 21; southern

Illinois (twelve years), February 26; central Missouri (fourteen years), February 26; Keokuk, Iowa (fourteen years), February 18; central Kansas (seven years), February 21; southern Nebraska (five years), February 23. Farther north average dates of arrival are Erie, Pa., March 11 (earliest February 23, 1891); northwestern New York, March 25 (earliest February 25, 1902); southern Ontario, April 18; Ottawa, Ontario, April 30; Montreal, April 23; Prince Edward Island, April 24. The late arrival of this species in eastern Canada is noteworthy, for by the time it reaches there, late April, in the interior it has penetrated a thousand miles farther north. Along this latter route average dates of appearance are southern Michigan, March 18; vicinity of Chicago (thirteen years), March 20 (earliest March 12, 1893). The normal time of arrival in central Iowa, as deduced from copious records for twenty years, seems to be March 6, but in twelve of these years one station or another reported unusually early birds, the average date of arrival of which is February 21. The average date when southern Minnesota is reached is (fourteen years) March 9 and northwestern Minnesota (four years) April 8. On the plains the average dates are, northern Nebraska, March 5; southern South Dakota, March 8; central South Dakota, March 17; Larimore, N. Dak., April 3 (earliest March 20, 1889); Reaburn, Manitoba, April 8 (earliest April 5, 1900); Qu'Appelle, Saskatchewan, April 10 (earliest March 25, 1905); Great Slave Lake, Mackenzie, about May 1; Fort Confidence, May 22, 1849. A very early bird was seen at Fort Simpson, Mackenzie, April 28, 1904. Nearer the Rocky Mountains, the average date at Terry, Mont., was April 1 (earliest March 10, 1902); Great Falls, Mont., March 16 (earliest March 10, 1889); Edmonton, Alberta, April 7, 1887; St. Michael and Nulato, Alaska, about May 1; Kowak River, Alaska, May 14, 1899; Point Barrow, Alaska, June 18, 1882.

The pintail not only migrates early, but it is also among the earlier ducks to breed, as evidenced by the following data: Will, Ill., eggs, May 10, 1877; Calumet Marsh, Illinois, fresh eggs, May 29, 1875; Hancock County, Iowa, eggs, May 1, 1879; Hay Lake, Nebraska, half-grown young, June 17, 1902; North Dakota, eggs, early May, young, first week of June; Oak Lake, Manitoba, incubated eggs, May 24, 1892; near Lake Athabasca, eggs nearly hatched, June 8, 1901; Nulato, Alaska, beginning to breed May 20; Circle City, Alaska, downy young, July 10, 1903; Kowak River, Alaska, first eggs, June 1, 1899.

Fall migration.—As is true of most ducks, there is a southward movement in August, but it is not until early September that many appear south of the breeding grounds, and in the course of two weeks a few birds find their way even to the Gulf of Mexico, arriving there by the middle of September. Some early dates are: Erie, Pa., September 6, 1893; Alexandria, Va., September 13, 1890; Long

Island, September 15, 1903; Rhode Island, September 4; eastern Massachusetts, September 11; Montreal, September 3. The main flight is a whole month later, bringing the birds in large numbers to Chesapeake Bay the middle of October and to the coast of North Carolina late in that month. Some very early migrants have been seen in west central Texas September 4; at Corpus Christi, Tex., August 18, 1902, and at the southern end of Lower California, August 29. The last ones leave the Arctic just about the time the first reach the Gulf of Mexico; the last were noted at Point Barrow, Alaska, September 7, 1882; Kowak River, Alaska, September 14, 1898; St. Michael, Alaska, October 10; Fort Franklin, Mackenzie, September 27, 1903. Large flocks begin to leave southern Minnesota the middle of October, and most have departed by the first of November.

[**Pœcilonetta bahamensis** (Linn.). Bahama Duck.

This duck is among the species that range most widely in the Western Hemisphere. It is strange that it should not have been detected in Florida, for it occurs throughout the Bahamas, even in the most northern islands. Thence it ranges through the Greater and the Lesser Antilles to South America. In Brazil it is one of the most abundant ducks and occurs in decreasing numbers even south to the Falkland Islands. It has been recorded from every country of South America except Colombia, Venezuela, and Ecuador. It breeds throughout its range from the Bahamas to the Falklands.]

Aix sponsa (Linn.). Wood Duck.

Breeding range.—The wood duck is more closely confined to the United States than any other North American duck. South of this country it is not a rare resident in Cuba and is accidental in Jamaica and the Bermudas. It occurs in California south to Los Angeles and Ventura counties, in the latter of which it breeds. There is a single record for Mexico, at Mazatlan. It breeds in eastern Texas, south rarely to San Antonio; thence to the Pacific slope and north throughout the whole Rocky Mountain region it is rare or accidental. It is recorded as breeding in southwestern Colorado (Fort Lewis), northern Idaho (Fort Sherman), northern Montana (Flathead Lake), and as a rare migrant in various localities south to New Mexico and Arizona.

The northern extension of its range is found in Nova Scotia and New Brunswick, for the species is not yet recorded from Newfoundland, and there seems to be no reliable record for Labrador. It ranges at least as far north as Montreal, Ottawa, Moose Factory, Trout Lake, and Cumberland House. It appears to be absent from the Rocky Mountain region of Canada, but occurs in southern British Columbia (Agassiz, Sumas, Chilliwack, and Burnaby Lake).

It is one of the earliest ducks to breed, as young were found in northern Florida on March 19, 1877.

Winter range.—The southern range in winter has already been given; northward the species winters regularly to North Carolina, occasionally in Maryland and Pennsylvania; accidentally in New York and Massachusetts. In the interior it is found at this season as far north as southern Indiana, southern Illinois, and Kansas. On the Pacific coast a few winter near the northern limit of the summer range.

Spring migration.—This duck is one of those which migrate north moderately early, and in central New York the average date of its arrival is March 25 (earliest March 16, 1898); eastern Massachusetts, March 24; Montreal, Canada, April 24; central Iowa, March 20 (earliest March 7, 1898); northern Ohio April 1 (earliest March 10, 1887); Petersburg, Mich., March 15; southern Ontario, April 17 (earliest April 1, 1890); Ottawa, Ontario (average fifteen years), April 22 (earliest March 26, 1898); Heron Lake, Minn., April 4 (earliest March 24, 1890); Elk River, Minn., April 6 (earliest April 4, 1885); southern Manitoba, April 15 (earliest April 2, 1895.)

Fall migration.—The southward migration amounts to no more than withdrawal from the northern half of the summer range. This occurs largely during October, and the average date when the last migrants are seen at Ottawa, Ontario (fourteen years), is October 27 (latest November 7, 1896); Montreal, November 1; southern Maine, October 27 (latest November 2, 1896); southern Iowa, November 9 (latest November 21.)

[Cairina moschata (Linn.). Muscovy Duck.

In its domesticated form this duck is well known throughout the civilized world. In its wild state it is an abundant inhabitant of Middle and South America from Tampico, Yucatan, Mazatlan, and the Rio Zacatula in Mexico to central Argentina. There is no certain record of its occurrence in the United States nor in the West Indies, although a supposed hybrid between the muscovy and the mallard was described from Jamaica under the name of *Anas maxima*, and similar birds have been taken several times along the Atlantic coast of the United States. Probably all these escaped from domestication.]

Netta rufina (Pall.). Rufous-crested Duck.

This is a European and Asiatic species, one specimen of which was found in 1872 in the New York City market.

Aythya americana (Eyt.). Redhead.

Breeding range.—The greater number of redheads summer in a rather restricted area in western central Canada, comprising western Manitoba, Alberta, and Saskatchewan. The species breeds not rarely in the northern portions of Minnesota, North Dakota, and Montana. It is less common in southern Minnesota (Madison, Heron Lake), southern South Dakota (Harrison, Vermilion), Idaho (Lake Hoodoo), and on the Pacific slope locally from Lac la Hache, British Columbia, south to southern California (Ventura and Los Angeles counties), and east to Ruby Lake, Nevada, and Rush Lake, Utah. The redhead used to breed not uncommonly in the great marshes of the lake region of southeastern Wisconsin, but now it is restricted to a few localities, one of which is Lake Koshkonong. It has bred on the St. Clair Flats of Michigan and Ontario.

Only a few pass as far north as 54° latitude, the northern range of the species thus being more restricted than that of any other Canadian duck. A stray was taken in 1896 on Kadiak Island, Alaska, the only record on the Pacific coast north of Vancouver Island, and an individual was taken in the fall in southeastern Labrador. It is not yet recorded in Newfoundland, and is a rare migrant in the Maritime Provinces.

Winter range.—The principal winter home of the redhead is from Texas, along the Gulf and Atlantic coasts, to Chesapeake Bay; a few winter on Long Island, and a still smaller number around Cape Cod and Lakes Ontario and Erie; the species winters in the Mississippi Valley north to Illinois and Kansas, and in the West to New Mexico, Arizona—rarely Utah—Nevada, and southern British Columbia, almost as far north as it breeds. The redhead is not uncommon in winter in the Valley of Mexico, but is quite rare on the west coast south to Manzanillo and southern Lower California. It is accidental in Jamaica.

Spring migration.—The redhead moves north with the great body of river ducks soon after the first open water appears. Average dates of arrival are: Oberlin, Ohio, March 10 (earliest March 4, 1904); central Indiana, March 13 (earliest March 6, 1887); southern Ontario, March 24 (earliest March 14, 1898); Keokuk, Iowa, March 7 (earliest February 13, 1898); central Iowa, March 18 (earliest, March 8, 1887); southern Wisconsin, March 30 (earliest March 10, 1898); Heron Lake, Minn., March 26; central Nebraska, March 10 (earliest February 10, 1896); northern Montana, April 13 (earliest April 7, 1895); southern Manitoba, April 21 (earliest April 12, 1903). Eggs have been found in southern California in May; at Horicon Lake, Wisconsin, May 24; in northern North Dakota, June 1; at Rush Lake, Saskatchewan, June 15.

Fall migration.—The movement of the redhead exhibits in extreme degree a phase of migration, shared to a lesser extent by several other species, in which the course taken is at a wide angle from the normal southern one. Lake Winnipeg marks the extreme northeastern part of the district where it breeds commonly, and yet the species is a fairly common fall migrant along the Atlantic coast from Cape Cod southward. The individuals that visit Cape Cod take an almost eastern course, or at least go 3 miles east for every mile south. From the nearest breeding grounds to the lower Hudson Valley, which is about as far north as the species occurs regularly in large numbers, the course is almost at right angles to the general trend of the Atlantic coast line. In other words, this is the course the redhead should take to reach salt water by the shortest route. This route from Manitoba to Long Island is through a district abounding in shallow lakes and marshes, which furnish abundant food. After reaching the coast, most of the redheads pass southward and winter from Chesapeake Bay to Florida and the Bahamas. Only a portion of the species, however, takes this east and west course. Many flocks pass directly south and are common all through the Mississippi Valley to the Gulf coast and through Texas to central Mexico. The average date when the first migrants appear in southern Ontario is September 19 (earliest September 10, 1896); at Erie, Pa., the average date is October 7, while at Alexandria, Va., a long series of careful records fixes October 12 as the average date of arrival—October 5 (1901) the earliest—and October 29 as the average date when the species becomes common. In general it may be said that the large flocks cross into North Dakota about the 1st of October, are common in the central Mississippi Valley about the middle of the month, and reach the Gulf coast, from Texas to Florida, early in November, when the last are deserting the northern breeding grounds.

A single individual was seen in southeastern Labrador, September 23, and this bird must have journeyed nearly 2,000 miles in a due easterly direction.

Aythya vallisneria (Wils.). Canvasback.

Breeding range.—The district just east of the Rocky Mountains in Alberta seems to be a center of abundance of this species in the breeding season. East of this district it breeds commonly to about the one hundredth meridian; south to the southern boundary of Canada, west to central British Columbia and Sitka, north to Great Slave Lake, and northwest to Gens de large Mountains and Fort Yukon. It does not commonly breed in the United States, but a few nest in northern North Dakota and in diminishing numbers southward to Nebraska (Cody, Irwin, Hackberry Lake); it is rare as a breeder in Minnesota (Madison, Heron Lake), and a few crippled birds have been known to breed on Lake Koshkonong, Wisconsin. In 1900 it bred casually at Barr Lake, near Denver, Colo., and it has been known to breed at Pyramid Lake, Nevada, and in a few places in Oregon.

Winter range.—The statements of the breeding range just made show that the eastern edge of the regular summer home is more than a thousand miles west of Chesapeake Bay, which, until a comparatively recent period, was a favorite winter home for the canvasback. The line of the Great Lakes seems to be the general route followed in this southeastward migration, and a few canvasbacks stop for the winter as far north as Lake Erie and western New York.   To the northward of Chesapeake Bay the numbers decrease rapidly until Long Island is reached, where the bird is rare.   It is hardly more than a straggler in Massachusetts and is accidental in Maine, New Brunswick, and Nova Scotia.   It has not been recorded as yet from Newfoundland, Labrador, or the Hudson Bay region.

The great flocks that formerly covered Chesapeake Bay are of the past, but a few still winter on the coast of the Carolinas.   Accidentals are recorded from the Bermudas, from Cuba and Jamaica, and one from Guatemala.   These seem to be all the records south of the Valley of Mexico, where it is not rare in winter.   The winter range extends from this district and Mazatlan on the western coast, north to southern Illinois, Colorado, Nevada, and southern British Columbia.

Spring migration.—In February a few move north, bringing the van the latter part of that month to about latitude 39° in the Mississippi Valley, which is the northern limit of the species in mild winters. Early March brings the species to southern Iowa.   Average dates of spring arrival are: Keokuk, Iowa, March 12; central Iowa, March 15; southern Wisconsin, March 26; Heron Lake, Minn., March 28 (earliest March 19, 1889); central Nebraska, March 14; northern North Dakota, April 18; southern Manitoba, April 21 (earliest April 6, 1885).   In the interior of British Columbia eggs have been found May 21; in North Dakota, May 18; at Great Slave Lake, June 4, and Fort Yukon, June 3.

Fall migration.—In the day of the great flights to Chesapeake Bay the gunners did not expect large flocks of canvasbacks much before the middle of November, but a small number appeared some time earlier.   For the last sixteen years the average date of the first arrival at Alexandria, Va., has been October 21 (earliest October 15, 1903). On the average canvasbacks have become tolerably common by November 8; in 1888 by the last of October.   These flocks cross Lake Erie early in October, and the height of the shooting season there is toward the end of that month.   The first flocks cross the boundary to the upper Mississippi Valley the last week in September and during the month of October spread gradually south to the southern limit of the range in the Valley of Mexico.   Southern California is reached about October 20.   In 1895 the last were seen at Heron Lake, Minnesota, on November 27.

Aythya marila (Linn.).   Scaup Duck; Broadbill; Blackhead; Bluebill.

Breeding range.—The principal summer home of the scaup in the Western Hemisphere is northwestern North America, from northern North Dakota, southeastern British Columbia, and Sitka, Alaska, north to Fort Churchill, Great Slave Lake, Fort Reliance, Alaska, and Kotzebue Sound; also throughout the whole Aleutian chain to the

Near Islands. It breeds accidentally or casually at Mount Vernon, Va., 1881; Magdalen Islands, Gulf of St. Lawrence; Toronto, Ontario; St. Clair Flats, Michigan; Clear Lake, Iowa; Minneapolis and Fergus Falls, Minn.; and Great Whale River, James Bay.

The species also breeds in the arctic regions of the Old World, and winters south to southern Europe and central Asia.

Winter range.—This is one of the principal game birds of the Atlantic coast region from Massachusetts to Chesapeake Bay, and it is probably more common here during the winter than in any other part of its range. The winter range on the Atlantic coast of this and the next species is complementary. The present species is common from Chesapeake Bay northward, while most of the lesser scaups winter south of that district and are most common from North Carolina to Florida. A small proportion of the flocks of the greater scaup pass south to the Carolinas and a few continue on to Florida and the Bahamas. The records for the West Indies seem to belong to the lesser scaup and the same is probably true of the few records for Mexico and Central America.

The species winters regularly on the New Jersey coast and usually on Long Island; its stay in Massachusetts is governed by winter conditions, and during mild winters like those of 1891–92, 1893–94, and 1903–4, it is quite common along the southeastern coast. Occasionally some scaups winter even on the coast of Maine. It occurs throughout the Mississippi Valley in winter north to southern Wisconsin and Toronto, Ontario, though it is hardly more than a straggler in winter north of the Ohio River.

The greater scaup ranges nearly to the southwestern boundary of the United States in southern Texas, southern New Mexico, central Arizona, and to San Diego, Cal. A few winter in southern Colorado, southern Utah, and more commonly in Nevada, and on the Pacific coast north to the Aleutian Islands.

Spring migration.—Few birds have a more pronounced northwest and southeast migration than the greater scaup duck. Its center of abundance in winter is on the Atlantic coast between the meridians of 74° and 76° longitude, but almost all of these Atlantic coast birds breed west of the meridian of 95° longitude, and their route in spring is along the general direction of the chain of lakes that stretches almost due northwestward from Lake Erie to Great Slave Lake. The two routes of migration—south along the Mississippi River and southwest to the New England coast—are revealed still more clearly in the fall, when this species scarcely occurs in Indiana, though common both to the east and west of that State. In spring some of the flocks move north along the coast, slightly beyond their winter home, to eastern Massachusetts, but so large a proportion of them turn inland that the species is rare to the northeastward of this State, straggling to Newfoundland, and once recorded on the eastern coast of Labrador. Average dates of spring arrival are: Montreal, Canada, April 15 (earliest April 7, 1893); Oberlin, Ohio, March 24 (earliest March 9, 1904); central Indiana, March 17 (earliest March 1, 1892); northern Illinois, March 23 (earliest March 6, 1894); southern Ontario, March 30; southern Michigan, March 29; southern Wisconsin, March 13; central Iowa, March 16; Heron Lake, Minn., April 2; southern Manitoba, April 16 (earliest March 31, 1892); in 1905 one was seen March 27 at Indian Head, Saskatchewan, nearly a month earlier than usual. The species was seen May 24, 1901, at Fort Chipewyan, Alberta, and the first was noted May 24, 1904, at Fort Simpson. Its arrival has been noted at Fort Reliance, Yukon, May 1; at St. Michael, Alaska, May 8–10, and on the Kowak River, Alaska, June 1, 1899.

In most seasons about Long Island the last week of March marks the disappearance of the large flocks. Some years they remain during the first few days of April, and the last linger until about the 1st of May.

Eggs have been taken at Minneapolis, Minn., May 13; Oak Lake, Manitoba, May 24, 1892; Kowak River, Alaska, June 14, 1899; St. Michael, Alaska, end of May.

Fall migration.—Soon after the first of October, flocks of 'broadbills' begin to appear near Long Island and the numbers increase all through this month. September 26 is the average date when the first scaups arrive. Early arrivals, on the average, reach Alexandria, Va., October 18, and the species becomes common about the 1st of November. October is the month of arrival for this species throughout most of its winter range in the United States, and the early part of this month is the time of departure from the most northern breeding grounds. The last leave St. Michael, Alaska, October 7 to 15. The last leave Montreal, on the average, November 9 (latest November 14, 1896); the latest was seen at Heron Lake, Minn., November 27, 1885.

Aythya affinis (Eyt.).   Lesser Scaup Duck.

Breeding range.—In the case of this species a distinction needs to be drawn between the breeding range and the summer range. Quite a number of nonbreeding individuals spend the summer many miles south of the nesting grounds, so that the eggs or young are the only certain evidence that the species breeds. These nonbreeding birds are not rare on the New England coast, Long Island Sound, and the Great Lakes. The lesser scaup does not breed regularly in northeastern United States nor in any of the Maritime Provinces; indeed, there is scarcely a breeding record for the whole of North America east of Hudson Bay and Lake Huron. The extreme easterly points at which the species breeds are around Lake St. Clair and the western end of Lake Erie in Ohio, Michigan, and Ontario; thence westward, a few breed in northern Indiana (Kewanna, English Lake), southern Wisconsin (Delavan, Lake Koshkonong), northern Iowa (Spirit Lake, Clear Lake), northern Nebraska (probably in Cherry County), Montana (common), and central British Columbia (Cariboo district). The species is rather rare on the Pacific coast and seems to have been found only once on the coast of Alaska (Portage Bay, near Chilkat River), though not rare inland on the Yukon River, breeding as far north as Circle City. The principal breeding range of the lesser scaup is the interior of Canada, from northern North Dakota and northern Montana to the edge of the timber near the Arctic coast in the Anderson River and the Mackenzie River regions.

Migration range.—The route of migration in the fall evidently tends toward the southeast, for at this season the species is not uncommon in New England, and is a rare visitant of Nova Scotia and even of Newfoundland, and is accidental in Greenland and the Bermudas.

Winter range.—The southeastward movement just mentioned brings a large number of lesser scaups to the South Atlantic States, from Maryland southward; indeed, in Florida it is one of the commonest ducks, and continues to be common as far south as the Bahamas, the Greater Antilles, and east to St. Croix, St. Thomas, Virgin Gorda, St. Lucia, and Trinidad. It is not rare in Panama and Costa Rica, while it is abundant in Guatemala, Yucatan, Mexico, and Lower California, and less common on the Pacific slope north to southern British Columbia. The species remains north in winter, on the Atlantic coast as far as New Jersey and Pennsylvania, and in the interior as far as southern Illinois, southern Colorado, and Arizona. There are a few records of its occurrence in winter in western New York.

Spring migration.—An abundant migrant in the upper Mississippi Valley, the lesser scaup is one of the less early ducks to arrive. It has appeared at Keokuk, Iowa, just north of its winter home, on February 26, average of five years (earliest date February 21, 1892); while during another period of five years the average date of its arrival was March 19. The average date of arrival in central Iowa is March 21, as deduced from thirteen years' observations; at Heron Lake, Minn., March 22 (earliest March 5, 1887); central Nebraska, March 29; Loveland, Colo., March 12 (earliest March 8, 1887). The average of six years' observations at Chicago, Ill., gives April 6 as the date of appearance, while in a neighboring locality, English Lake, Ind., it has been taken several times by March 12, and in 1892 on March 6. The average dates are: Central Indiana, March 27; Oberlin, Ohio, March 23 (earliest March 15, 1901); southern Michigan, March 25 (earliest March 11, 1905); Ottawa, Ontario, April 26; Montreal, Canada, April 14; Reaburn, Manitoba, April 9. This species was seen near Pelican Rapids, Alberta, May 7, 1901, and at Fort Simpson, Mackenzie, May 24, 1904. It is one of the later breeding ducks. Young were seen at Mitchells Bay, Ontario, June 6, 1888; eggs at Rush Lake, Saskatchewan, May 28, 1892; and eggs on the lower Anderson June 17, 1865.

Fall migration.—The species remains on its breeding grounds until quite late in the fall, and in the United States rarely becomes numerous before the 1st of October. At Alexandria, Va., the average date of arrival (ten years) is October 12 (earliest, September 25, 1903) and the average date on which it becomes common is October 27. In 1902 the first arrival in northern Florida was seen November 18, and about this date it appears in the Bahamas and in southern Lower California. It is one of the last of the river ducks to leave the far north, and in 1903 was seen at latitude 64° on the Mackenzie River until the middle of October. Average dates when the last were seen are: Montreal, Canada, November 5 (latest, November 12, 1894); Ottawa, Ontario, November 11 (latest, November 21, 1892); southern Manitoba, November 8; southern Minnesota, November 13; Keokuk, Iowa, December 2.

Aythya collaris (Donov.).   Ring-necked Duck.

Breeding range.—The summer home of this species seems to comprise two general areas separated by the Rocky Mountains. The greater number breed in the interior, from North Dakota and Minnesota north to Athabasca Lake and east to the western side of Lake Winnipeg. It breeds rarely south to southern Minnesota (Minneapolis, Heron Lake), northern Iowa (Clear Lake), and to southern Wisconsin (Lake Koshkonong; Pewaukee Lake). Though eventually the species may be found breeding in Alberta, at present there seems to be no certain nesting record for the entire Rocky Mountain chain from New Mexico to Alberta. West of the Rockies the ring-necked duck seems to breed in small numbers from Fort Klamath, Oreg., to southern British Columbia (Cariboo district). It is said to breed also on the Near Islands, Alaska.

Winter range.—The Gulf coast, from Florida to Texas, is the principal winter home of the ring-necked duck, and here locally it is the most abundant duck at this season. It is common also in the Bahamas and Cuba, rare in Jamaica, and has been noted once in Porto Rico, and once in the Bermudas. On the mainland it is rare in California and Lower California, common in Mexico, and ranges to central Guatemala. Northward it is common in the Carolinas, rare to Maryland and New Jersey, and thence westward to southern Illinois, northern Texas, New Mexico, and north on the Pacific coast to southern British Columbia.

Spring migration.—Along the Atlantic coast from Massachusetts northward to Newfoundland this species is a rare migrant, and is one of the later ducks to move. The average date of arrival at Erie,

Pa., is April 16 (earliest March 15, 1903). The migration in the Mississippi Valley is somewhat earlier; average dates are: English Lake, Ind., March 11 (earliest February 27, 1892); Keokuk, Iowa, March 14 (earliest March 4, 1894); Heron Lake, Minn., March 27 (earliest March 15, 1894). The first arrival was noted at Osler, Saskatchewan, May 2, 1893, and at Fort Chipewyan May 22, 1893. Eggs have been taken at Pewaukee Lake, Wisconsin, May 20, 1867; Minneapolis, Minn., May 27, 1876; Turtle Mountain, N. Dak., June 14, 1898; Rush Lake, Saskatchewan, June 15, 1892.

Fall migration.—Southward migration in the Mississippi Valley is earlier than it is along the Atlantic coast; in the former the bird reaches the Gulf coast about the middle of September, and has been noted in the Valley of Mexico September 28; along the Atlantic it appears at Alexandria, Va., on the average, October 23 (earliest arrival October 6, 1901), and it becomes common at an average date of November 11. It was seen near Athabasca Landing September 4, 1903. The average date when the last migrants were seen at Ottawa, Ontario, was October 30 (latest November 21, 1892); latest in Massachusetts November 23; Erie, Pa., December 3, average date of the last arrivals in southern Minnesota (eight years) November 13.

Clangula clangula americana (Bonap.). American Golden-eye.

Breeding range.—This is one of the more northern-breeding ducks, but its choice of hollow trees as nesting sites prevents the extension of its breeding range into the treeless Arctic regions, to which it seems well suited by its hardy constitution. It has been noted north to Ungava Bay, Labrador; Fort Churchill, Hudson Bay; and Fort Good Hope, near the mouth of the Mackenzie River. It is probable that the species breeds in the heavy timber nearest to these places. In Alaska it breeds commonly in the interior about as far north as the Arctic Circle, but is very rarely seen on the coast. The species breeds from Newfoundland to British Columbia, north to the Noatak River, but the breeding range extends only a little into the United States, to southern Maine (Calais, Magalloway River), northern New Hampshire (Lake Umbagog), northern Vermont (St. Johnsbury), northern New York (Adirondacks), northern Michigan (Neebish Island, Sault Ste. Marie), North Dakota (Devils Lake), Montana (Flathead Lake), and in British Columbia so close to the southern boundary that the species will probably be found to breed in northern Washington.

The typical form, *Clangula clangula*, breeds in northern Europe and northern Asia, migrating southward to northern Africa and southern Asia.

Winter range.—As this is one of the hardiest ducks, its northern distribution in winter is governed by the presence of open water. It is tolerably common on Lakes Michigan, Erie, and Ontario, and in mild winters, as that of 1888–89, it remains north to Prince Edward Island. It is common in winter all along the New England coast, and continues to be common to North Carolina, less common in South Carolina, and rare or accidental to the southward. All records for the West Indies seem to be erroneous. It was once seen at sea near the Bahamas, has been taken a few times in the Bermudas, and has been seen a few times in Florida; it is not rare at the mouth of the Mississippi River, but is quite rare in Texas and New Mexico, is recorded in Mexico (Mazatlan and northeastern Lower California), and is rare in southern California. In the interior it remains during the winter north to Iowa, Nebraska, and Utah, while on the Pacific coast it is found at this season north to the Aleutian Islands.

Spring migration.—The spring records of this species are very irregular, as might be expected from its habit of wintering far north near large bodies of water. Observers on the coast of Maine report it as common all winter, while inland in southern Maine the first was not seen (average eight years) until April 5 (earliest March 27, 1902); at Montreal, Canada (average nine years), April 4 (earliest March 19, 1894); North River, Prince Edward Island, April 8, and at Lake Mistassini, Quebec, May 3, 1885. At Ottawa, Ontario, it was one of the most irregular birds in its arrival. In twelve years out of eighteeen the first arrival was not noted until April, average April 12; for five years the first came in March, and in 1885 the first was seen February 14. Other average dates of arrival are: Southern Ontario, April 5; northern Iowa, March 21; Heron Lake, Minn., March 25 (earliest March 14, 1889); northern North Dakota, April 20; southern Manitoba, April 21 (earliest March 29, 1902). The first golden-eyes have been noted at Great Falls, Mont., March 9–22; central Alberta, April 7–17; Osler, Saskatchewan, May 2, 1893; Fort Resolution, Mackenzie, May 7, 1860, and Nulato, Alaska, May 3, 1868. An unusually early bird was seen on April 28, 1904, at Fort Simpson, Mackenzie. Eggs have been taken at Devils Lake, N. Dak., May 25, 1903; near Lake Athabasca June 6, 1903; downy young at Reaburn, Manitoba, July 4, 1893, and well-grown young June 23, 1894, near Ottawa, Ontario.

Fall migration.—The golden-eye is one of the late ducks to migrate southward, seldom appearing south of its breeding range before October and usually not until the latter part of that month. A long series of excellent notes at Alexandria, Va., shows the average date of arrival to be October 26 (earliest, October 8, 1901); on the average the species did not become common until November 11. The average date of appearance at Woods Hole, Mass., is November 15 and at Keokuk, Iowa, November 24. The average date when the last were seen at Montreal, Canada, is November 7.

Clangula islandica (Gmel.).   Barrow Golden-eye.

Breeding range.—A few breed in eastern Canada from the Gulf of Saint Lawrence (Point des Monts) to northern Labrador (Davis Inlet). A few are found in Greenland during March and April and in November and December as far north as Holstenborg, 67° latitude, but the species apparently does not breed there, though breeding quite commonly in Iceland.   The principal summer home is in the Rocky Mountains, where the species breeds from southern Colorado (Dolores County) north almost to the Arctic coast (Fort Anderson), though north of the United States there are only a few records in the entire district.   On the Pacific slope the species breeds quite commonly in central British Columbia and less commonly north to Lake Clark, Alaska.   The most southern record of breeding on the Pacific slope seems to be the one made by one of the parties of the Biological Survey at Paulina and Diamond lakes, Oregon.

Winter range.—The larger number of the breeding birds of eastern Canada spend the winter around the Gulf of St. Lawrence, but a few straggle south and have been recorded at this season from Maine, New Hampshire, Massachusetts, New York, Virginia, and on four occasions from North Carolina.   In the interior they have been recorded a few times in the States around the Great Lakes and even in Nebraska. The Rocky Mountain breeding birds pass in winter scarcely south of their summer range and are found from southern Colorado (Fort Lewis) to Montana (Fort Sherman and Great Falls).   The Pacific birds winter from southern Alaska (Portage Bay) to California (San Francisco).

Spring migration.—Records of this species are too few to allow of exact statements in regard to its migration; indeed, over most of the range of the species the winter and summer homes overlap.   Migrants were noted at Quebec City, April 14, 1899, and April 16, 1904.   One was seen near Asheville, N. C., in 1893 as late as May 6.   One was taken at Fort Anderson, Mackenzie, June 14, 1864.

In Iceland the species begins breeding in May or early June.   At Godbout, Quebec, young were found July 11, 1881.   Incubated eggs were taken June 17 in central British Columbia.

Fall migration.—The earliest fall migrants in 1897 at Montreal were seen October 23.   One was taken near Washington, D. C., November 22, 1889, and one at Lake Koshkonong, Wisconsin, November 14, 1896.

Charitonetta albeola (Linn.).   Buffle-head.

Breeding range.—In the nesting season the buffle-head is almost wholly confined to Canada, but a few breed in Wisconsin (Pewaukee Lake), northern Iowa (Storm, Clear, and Spirit lakes), Wyoming (Meeteetse Creek), Montana (Milk River, Flathead Lake).   It is a tolerably common breeder in the northern two-thirds of Ontario, and undoubtedly some pairs breed in Quebec and southern Labrador, though it is as yet unrecorded from there, from the Maritime Provinces, and from Newfoundland, except as a rather rare visitant.   In Manitoba and westward to British Columbia it becomes more common as a breeder, and ranges north to Fort Churchill, Fort Rae, the mouth of the Mackenzie, and the upper Yukon, rarely to the Yukon mouth. It has been taken as a rare straggler on the west coast of Greenland (Godhaven, October; Frederikshaab), and a few times in Europe.

Winter range.—A single specimen was found in the market at Habana, and this constitutes the only record south of the eastern United States.   To the westward a few enter Mexico to the Valley of Mexico and Lower California to San Quentin.   It is a common winter resident of the southern half of the United States, north to Massachusetts; Lakes Ontario, Huron, and Michigan; Utah, Idaho, British Columbia, Unalaska Island, and the Near Islands.   It is casual in winter in the Bermudas and there is one record from the Commander Islands, Kamchatka.

Spring migration.—As with most of the hardy ducks, spring migration begins in February, and by the middle of March the buffle-head is fairly common in the district where it winters only locally and during exceptionally mild seasons.   Average dates of arrival are: Renovo, Pa., March 18 (earliest February 29, 1904); New Brunswick and Nova Scotia, March 22; central Indiana, March 2; northern Illinois, March 21; southern Michigan, March 31 (earliest March 1, 1887); southern Ontario, April 7 (earliest April 1, 1903); Ottawa, Ontario, April 24 (earliest March 26, 1898); southern Iowa, March 22 (earliest March 1, 1891); Heron Lake, Minn., March 26 (earliest March 6, 1889); southeastern Minnesota, April 5; Elk River, Minn., April 11; central South Dakota, April 8; southern Manitoba, April 25; Osler, Saskatchewan, May 2, 1893; Fort Simpson, Mackenzie, May 11, 1904. Eggs have been taken at Fort Simpson May 25, 1860, and at Fort Yukon, June 7, 1862.

Fall migration.—This species is late in entering the United States, September records being rare, except in the extreme northern part, and even here the species is scarcely common before the middle of October.   At Renovo, Pa., the average date of arrival is November 10, though in 1901 the first was seen September 21.   The average date of the last migrants at Montreal was November 1, and at Ottawa, Ontario, November 8.   One was taken at Fort Reliance, on the upper Yukon, October 7.

Harelda hyemalis (Linn.).   Old-squaw.

Breeding range.—The summer home of this species includes the Arctic coasts and most of the islands.   It is abundant to the northern part of Banks Land and thence east to North Somerset Island and the south shore of Lancaster Sound—that is, to about latitude 74°. On the western coast of Greenland it is common to about latitude 72°. A few pass much farther north to Melville Island, Wellington Channel, and along the whole western coast of Greenland and on Grinnell Land to at least latitude 82°. The old-squaw breeds south to the southeastern coast of Labrador, to Cape Fullerton on the west side of Hudson Bay and probably to Cape Jones on the eastern coast. Along the whole coast of the mainland from Hudson Bay to Alaska it breeds in enormous numbers, and is a common breeder on the Alaskan coast to the Aleutian and Near islands and on the Asiatic coast to the Commander Islands. The species breeds in the Arctic regions of the Old World and winters south to southern Europe and central Asia.

Winter range.—Old-squaws are common south to Chesapeake Bay and not rare as far south as the coast of North Carolina. So abundant are they on the New England coast that near Newport, R. I., in February, 1899, a flock was seen that was estimated to contain at least 50,000. During the winter of 1887–88, a few were noted at Charleston, S. C., and during the severe winter of 1894–95, flocks were seen off the coast of South Carolina. There are two records for Florida—near Titusville and in Leon County. In mild winters old-squaws remain in the Gulf of St. Lawrence, and some occur at this season in southern Greenland. They winter abundantly on the Great Lakes, and have been noted as casual visitors at St. Louis, Mo., April 1, November 20, and March 14; New Orleans, La., February 28, 1885, and February 13, 1899; Nebraska (Omaha, Neligh), Kansas (Patterson Lake, Gantz Mill), and Colorado (Fort Collins, Longmont, Denver). This species winters on the Pacific coast from the Aleutian Islands southward; it is tolerably common to the coast of Washington, and not rare to northern California; it is casual in southern California as far south as San Diego Bay.

Spring migration.—The principal movements of old-squaws along the New England coast are in April, and this is the time also when the species migrates through western Pennsylvania and western New York. The first of those that have moved south reappear at Grand Manan, New Brunswick, on an average date of March 9, and at Godbout, Quebec, April 22. North of its winter quarters it is one of the earliest ducks to arrive, and has been noted at Fort Simpson, Mackenzie, 62°, May 10, 1904; Winter Island, latitude 66°, May 3, 1822; Igloolik, latitude 69°, May 21, 1823; Boothia Felix, latitude 70°, June 12, 1830, June 20, 1831, about June 16, 1833, and not until after June 25, 1832; Prince of Wales Strait, latitude 75°, May 31, 1851; Mercy Bay, June 13, 1852; Winter Harbor, latitude 75°, June 22, 1820; Cape Sabine, latitude 78°, June 1, 1884; Van Rensselaer Harbor, latitude 79°, June 16, 1854; Fort Conger, latitude 81°, June 17, 1882, June 6, 1883; Floeberg Beach, latitude 82° 40', July 12, 1876. The last usually leave the eastern United States about the 1st of May (Erie, Pa., May 18, 1900). The last were seen at Fort McMurray, Alberta, May 15, 1901. On the Pacific coast, the first old-squaws were noted at Chilcat, Alaska, March 11, 1882; off the mouth of the Yukon, stragglers usually arrive early in April as soon as open water appears; the main migration is several weeks later, and the first arrivals appear at Point Barrow late in May (May 18, 1882; May 24, 1883; May 31, 1898). The first reached the mouth of the Kowak River, Alaska, May 22, 1899.

Eggs have been taken at St. Michael, May 18; on the Pribilof Islands, June 12; near the Kowak River the last of June; Fort Anderson, Mackenzie, June 7, 1864, June 14, 1865; northwestern Hudson Bay, June 27; Ungava Bay, Labrador, June 16.

Fall migration.—Fall migration had already begun and large flocks had passed south to Great Bear Lake in 1903 by August 28, and were still numerous there September 17. An unusually early migrant was seen near Erie, Pa., September 13, 1876. Early dates are September 30, 1895, on the coast of Massachusetts, and October 8, 1885, on Long Island. The average date of arrival for six years on the coast of Massachusetts is October 11, and for nine years on Long Island, October 16. The birds are most abundant the first half of November, after which month the larger number pass on to more southern waters. The last were seen near northern Greenland, latitude 82°, September 16, 1875. Most leave Point Barrow in early October, but a straggler was seen there December 9, 1882. They leave the coast of Alaska, off St. Michael, from the 15th to the 20th of October.

Histrionicus histrionicus (Linn.).   Harlequin Duck.

Breeding range.—The harlequin breeds commonly in Newfoundland and on the whole west coast of Greenland south of Upernavik, latitude 72°, on the east coast north to Scoresby Sound, and in Iceland; also along the north coast of Labrador, at Ungava Bay, and Hudson Strait. There is no reason for doubting that its breeding range is continuous from northern Labrador west to the mouth of the Mackenzie River, though breeding records from this region are wanting. The species was noted by one of the parties of the Biological Survey August 20 and 24, 1903, a short distance south of MacTavish Bay, Great Bear Lake, in latitude 65° 30′, where it was probably breeding. It has been taken also at Fort Rae, at Fort Simpson, and on Bear Lake River. It is known to breed from the mouth of the Mackenzie west to Kotzebue Sound and to the Siberian coast. It occurs in summer on most of the islands west of Alaska, south to the Shumagin Islands, and in the Aleutian chain west to the Near Islands and to the Commander Islands off the coast of Asia. Most, if not all, of these birds, however, are nonbreeders. It has been noted breeding at several localities in the interior of Alaska, and breeds locally throughout the mountainous region of western North America south to southwestern Colorado and to central California at about latitude 38°.

Winter range.—The harlequin is not rare at this season in the southern part of the Gulf of St. Lawrence, and thence is less common to Long Island Sound; it is accidental on the New Jersey coast, and once, March 20, 1886, has been noted at Pensacola, Fla. It is not uncommon in winter on Lake Michigan; an accidental was noted October 29 near St. Louis. It winters in Colorado at the southern limit of its breeding range but at several thousand feet lower altitude. On the Pacific coast it winters abundantly in the Aleutians and the Pribilof Islands; west to the Near Islands, the Commander Islands, and rarely to Japan; also along the coast of California to Monterey and in the interior to about 36° latitude (near Crockers Station). Accidental in Europe.

Spring migration.—The few individuals that winter on the Atlantic coast of the United States retire northward in January and early February, but some linger just south of the breeding grounds in the Gulf of St. Lawrence until late May. The species arrives on the coast of Greenland in March. On the Pacific coast the winter and breeding ranges so overlap that no regular progression northward can be distinguished. Migratory movements are noticeable on the coast of Oregon the last of March; the species was noted at Fort Simpson, Mackenzie, May 25, 1904; the van usually arrives at the mouth of the Yukon about the 1st of June.

Fall migration.—The first arrivals off the coast of Massachusetts do not appear until about the beginning of November, when the last are leaving the Greenland breeding grounds. The first arrivals have been noted at Toronto, Ontario, October 20, 1894, and at Omaha, Nebr. (accidental), September 16, 1893; September 19, 1895.

Camptolaimus labradorius (Gmel.).   Labrador Duck.

This is an extinct species, which within the last century nested from Labrador northward. During the winter it visited the coast of New England and passed as far south as Long Island and New Jersey, possibly to Chesapeake Bay. So far as known the last survivor was captured in 1871 at Grand Manan, New Brunswick. Forty-three specimens are known to be in museums.

Polysticta stelleri (Pall.).   Steller Eider.

Breeding range.—The principal summer home of this duck is along the northern coast of Siberia, where the species is enormously abundant. Thence it breeds on the eastern coast and islands south to the Near Islands, Unalaska, and the Shumagins. Eggs have been found at Unalaska May 18, in northern Siberia June 25, and downy young at Point Barrow, Alaska, July 28.

Winter range.—The Steller eider winters abundantly on the Near Islands and as far north as Unalaska, the Shumagins, and the Kenai Peninsula. The winter range extends south on the Asiatic coast to the Kurile Islands.

Spring migration.—The northward migration is limited chiefly to May. The first arrivals have been noted at Point Barrow June 5, 1882, June 11, 1883, June 9, 1898. During migration the species is fairly common along the coast of Alaska at Bristol Bay, the mouth of the Yukon, and in Norton Sound.

Fall migration.—The first arrival in the fall has been noted at St. Michael, Alaska, September 21. The southern limit of the winter home is reached about the 1st of November. The latest date at Point Barrow is September 17, and the last migrants leave St. Michael about the middle of October.

The Steller eider has occurred accidentally at Disco Bay, Greenland, in the fall of 1878; at Godbout, Quebec, February 17, 1898, and also at Point des Monts, Quebec.

Arctonetta fischeri (Brandt).   Spectacled Eider.

Breeding range.—The spectacled eider has a more restricted range than any other of the family. It breeds north to Point Barrow, Alaska, and thence along the coast to the mouth of the Kuskokwim River. The range extends also along the northern coast of Siberia to the mouth of the Lena, but the species has not as yet been taken breeding on the Asiatic side. By far the greater number of individuals nest around Norton Sound.

Winter range.—Winter records are almost wanting; the species has been noted at this season on the Near Islands and Unalaska, and it is probable that the Aleutian chain constitutes the principal winter home.

Spring migration.—The breeding grounds are reached in May, the earliest record at Norton Sound being May 6, and the usual date a week or more later. The first have been noted at Point Barrow May 29, 1882, May 26, 1883, and May 31, 1898.

Fresh eggs have been found at St. Michael June 10, and newly hatched young July 23; downy young were secured at Point Barrow July 28, 1898.

Fall migration.—The latest records at Point Barrow are August 24, 1883, and September 17, 1897. During this latter month all the breeding grounds from Norton Sound northward are deserted.

Somateria mollissima borealis (C. L. Brehm).   Northern Eider.

Breeding range.—This eider breeds in northeastern North America, south to Hamilton Inlet, Labrador, about latitude 54°; west to Southampton Island and Cape Fullerton, latitude 63°; north on the east coast of Greenland to Shannon Island, latitude 75°, and on the west coast to Dumb-bell Bay, latitude 82°; not abundant north of about 78° latitude. There is a lack of definite knowledge concerning the western limits of the range of this species. It is certain that the eiders of Hudson Bay, west to longitude 87°, belong to this form. It is also certain that the common eider on the Arctic coast of northwestern North America is *S. v-nigra*, and that this form occurs east along the coast of the mainland to about the mouth of the Coppermine River, 115° longitude. There seems to be no specimen of either form in any collection from the Arctic islands west of Baffin Bay. It is a fair presumption that the eiders of Wellington Channel and vicinity—longitude 90°–95°, where the species is common north to 77° latitude—belong to the eastern form and that those of Banks Land, longitude 115°–125°, are *S. v-nigra*, but the dividing line between the two forms remains to be determined. The typical form, *Somateria mollissima*, breeds in northwestern Europe and comes south in winter rarely to southern Europe.

Winter range.—In winter the northern eider ranges from southern Greenland and northern Hudson Bay south on the Atlantic coast to Massachusetts.

Spring migration.—Just north of the winter range, at Cumberland Sound, latitude 66°, the first appeared April 30, 1878; in Wellington Channel, latitude 76°, May 17, 1851; at Cape Sabine, latitude 79°, May 28, 1884; and at Thank God Harbor, latitude 81°, June 4, 1872.

The latest stragglers on the coast of New England leave the first week in April. The first eggs on Cumberland Sound were found June 21, 1878; the first at the south end of Greenland, June 24, 1886.

Fall migration.—The earliest migrants arrive on the coast of Massachusetts the last of October; the last were seen at Dumb-bell Bay, September 5, 1875; at Thank God Harbor, November 4, 1872; and in Cumberland Sound, November 17, 1878.

Somateria dresseri Sharpe. American Eider.

Breeding range.—The American eider rarely breeds on the coast of Maine; formerly its breeding range extended to the western side of Penobscot Bay, but is now restricted to a few colonies in Jericho Bay and on Old Man Island; it breeds abundantly on the shores of the Gulf of St. Lawrence and is fairly common north to the mouth of Hamilton Inlet, latitude 54°; it breeds commonly on the east shore of Hudson Bay, from latitude 54° to latitude 56°, and on the west shore in the vicinity of Fort Churchill.

Winter range.—The American eider winters as far north as Newfoundland; is common in the Gulf of St. Lawrence through the winter, and is not uncommon as far south as the Massachusetts coast: it is casual on the New Jersey coast, and is accidental near Marshall Hall, Md., and near Cobbs Island, Virginia (December 28, 1900). In the interior it has occurred on the Great Lakes; at Ottawa, Ontario; Licking Reservoir, Ohio; Lake Koshkonong, Wisconsin; and Loveland, Colo.

Spring migration.—After severe winters, when they have been driven away by the ice, American eiders return to Prince Edward Island about the last week in March and to Newfoundland the first of April. The last are seen on the Massachusetts coast in April (April 18, 1890; April 20, 1891; April 12, 1893; April 20, 1894; an unusually late bird was seen May 18, 1892). Eggs were found at Grand Manan, New Brunswick, May 31, 1833, and young on the south coast of Labrador July 4, 1860.

Fall migration.—They first appear off the Massachusetts coast early in November, occasionally in October (October 10, 1890; October 30, 1892), and are common by the end of November.

Somateria v-nigra Gray. Pacific Eider.

Breeding range.—The principal summer home of this eider is on the coasts and islands of Bering Sea and along the coast of the Arctic Ocean between the mouths of the Mackenzie and the Coppermine rivers. The species breeds west to the northeastern coast of Siberia and south to Cook Inlet, Kadiak Island, the Aleutians, Near, and Commander islands; it is accidental in the interior at Great Slave Lake and at Lawrence, Kans. It is probable that the eiders so abundant on Banks Land belong to this form and that a few range north to Melville Island.

Winter range.—The species seems to be massed during winter at the southern portion of the breeding range in the vicinity of the Aleutians.

Spring migration.—Early arrivals are sometimes seen near the mouth of the Yukon the last of April, but usually they appear about May 10. At Point Barrow the dates of arrival are May 16, 1882, and May 19, 1883. On the Kowak River eggs were found June 2, and the young appear about the first of July. Incubation seems to be simultaneous over all the district from the mouth of the Yukon to that of the Anderson.

Fall migration.—Pacific eiders seem to disappear from all points in their summer haunts at about the same time, the first week in October, but for several weeks previously numbers migrate along the north coast of Alaska. Many individuals winter and summer in the same locality, while the birds breeding about the mouth of the Coppermine River migrate at least 2,000 miles.

Somateria spectabilis (Linn.). King Eider.

Breeding range.—The king eider breeds in the arctic regions. It is abundant on the west coast of Greenland, breeding from latitude 66° north as far as land goes, to at least latitude 82° 30′; south to Nachvak,

Labrador, latitude 59°; Southampton Island, Hudson Bay, latitude 63°; west along the Arctic coast to Icy Cape and Point Barrow, to St. Lawrence Island in Bering Sea, and on the whole coast of northern Siberia. It seems to be rather rare in northeastern Europe. It is abundant on the arctic islands north at least to Melville Island, latitude 76°, and to the same latitude in Wellington Channel.

Winter range.—This species winters as far north as open water can be found, at least to southern Greenland. It is common during the winter in the Gulf of St. Lawrence, whence a few stray each winter to Long Island Sound and the New Jersey coast; casual at Cape Charles, Va., January 2, 1897; Ossabaw Island, Georgia, December 1, 1904; St. Catherine Island, Georgia, December 3, 1904; Brunswick, Ga., April 25 and May 5, 1890.

The species has been noted occasionally in the interior on Lakes Cayuga, Oneida, Ontario, Erie, and Michigan. The Pacific birds winter abundantly in the Aleutians, south to the Shumagin and Kadiak islands; accidental near San Francisco, winter of 1879.

Spring migration.—Even as far north as Greenland migratory movements of the king eider are noticed in early February; the first arrival was noted at Igloolik, latitude 69°, April 16, 1823; Wellington Channel, latitude 76°, June 9, 1851; vicinity of Fort Conger, latitude 82°, June 12, 1872; June 16, 1882; June 11, 1883. The Pacific birds arrived at Point Barrow, latitude 71°, April 27, 1882, and May 5, 1883; eggs, Floeberg Beach, latitude 82° 30', July 9, 1876. The last breeding birds desert southern Greenland late in April, though non-breeders are not rare through the summer, and it is probably the presence of these that has given rise to reports that the species breeds in the Gulf of St. Lawrence; late birds have been recorded on the Massachusetts coast April 5, 1890; April 10, 1893; April 12, 1894; on Long Island April 21, 1887, and, as already noted, at Brunswick, Ga., May 5, 1890.

Fall migration.—This eider wanders south in late fall, the average date when it arrives on the coast of Massachusetts and Long Island being November 14 (earliest, October 21, 1899); it was noted on Lake Erie November 13, 1894, and at Calgary, Alberta, November 4, 1894. The height of the fall migration at Point Barrow is during September and October, and in 1882 the last one was seen there December 2, off St. Michael October 12, 1879, and at Fort Simpson, Mackenzie, October 25, 1903.

Oidemia americana Sw. & Rich. American Scoter.

Breeding range.—The lack of information in regard to the breeding of this species in northeastern North America is surprising. The species was described from the west shore of Hudson Bay, and occurs on the coasts of Labrador and the Gulf of St. Lawrence, but there seems to be no record of the discovery of the nest in this region. Nonbreeding birds are known to occur far south of the breeding grounds. The species is unknown from the whole vast interior of North America, between Hudson Bay on the east and the Yukon Valley on the west, and south almost to the United States boundary; it ranges north to Ungava Bay, Hudson Strait, and Fort Churchill, Hudson Bay, and apparently does not breed south of Newfoundland, nor in Labrador south of about latitude 52°; so that it follows by exclusion that the multitudes of these ducks that winter from the Gulf of St. Lawrence south along the Atlantic coast must breed in northern Ungava.

The American scoter is much more abundant on the Pacific coast, and breeds from the Aleutians and Near Island north to Kotzebue Sound and northeastern Asia.

Winter range.—The American scoter remains in winter around Newfoundland, except when it is driven away by the drift ice; thence south it is not uncommon to Long Island Sound and the coast of New Jersey, less common to South Carolina, rare or accidental in Florida; it is not rare on the Great Lakes during the winter, and has been observed at various places inland in the neighboring States; rare or accidental at St. Louis, Mo.; Lake Catherine, Louisiana; Lincoln, Nebr.; Fort Collins, Colo.; and Cheyenne, Wyo. The Pacific birds winter from the Aleutian Islands to the Santa Barbara Islands, California, and also to Japan on the Asiatic side.

Spring migration.—Arrivals from the south appear in the Gulf of St. Lawrence from March 25 to the first week in April, and the breeding grounds are reached soon after the middle of May. Most of the birds disappear from the coast of Massachusetts the last week of April, but belated individuals have been seen at Cobb Island, Virginia, May 19, 1891; Shelter Island, N. Y., June 5, 1893; and Woods Hole, Mass., June 10, 1891. On the Pacific side the first arrivals were noted at St. Michael, Alaska, May 16, and in Kotzebue Sound June 3. A few linger on the Pacific coast of the United States until early May.

Fall migration.—An American scoter was noted at Black River, Lewis County, N. Y., September 27, 1877; one at Ottawa, Ontario, September 21, 1887, and one at Woods Hole, Mass., September 9, 1891, but the regular flight does not occur until early October, and at about the same time the first migrants are seen on the coast of Puget Sound. The last ones leave St. Michael, Alaska, from the 10th to 15th of October.

Oidemia fusca (Linn.).   Velvet Scoter.

This is an Asiatic and European species, an individual of which was taken in May, 1878, near Godthaab, on the western coast of Greenland.

Oidemia deglandi Bonap. White-winged Scoter.

Breeding range.—This scoter breeds along the north shore of the Gulf of St. Lawrence and north to Nachvak Bay, Labrador, about latitude 59°; in the interior it breeds in North Dakota (Devils Lake), Manitoba, Alberta, and north to Hudson Bay and the Arctic coast. On the Pacific coast it breeds from British Columbia (158-Mile House) north to Kotzebue Sound and the coast of northeastern Siberia, rarely to Point Barrow. It is not common anywhere in Alaska. Nonbreeders remain as far south in summer as the coast of California and are not uncommon along the New England coast south to Rhode Island.

Winter range.—The Gulf of St. Lawrence and south along the Atlantic coast to South Carolina—accidental in Florida—constitutes the winter range. The species is especially common on the coast of Massachusetts and Long Island Sound. In the interior it extends its range south regularly and commonly to the Great Lakes; less commonly to the smaller bodies of water in the neighboring States; casually to Louisiana, Illinois (opposite St. Louis), Iowa (Lost Island Lake), Nebraska (Omaha, Lincoln), Colorado (Fort Collins, Loveland, Longmont, Denver). It winters on the Pacific coast from Unalaska Island to San Quentin Bay, Lower California.

Spring migration.—Early northward movements on the New England coast begin late in March, and at about this time the first migrants appear in the Gulf of St. Lawrence; the principal flights occur from the middle of April to the first week in May. At Heron Lake, Minn., where the species does not winter, the first were noted April 6, 1888; March 21, 1889; April 5, 1890, and April 9, 1891; at Aweme, Manitoba, April 27, 1897; April 15, 1898, and April 22, 1899. In the Devils Lake region of North Dakota the earliest eggs are laid about the middle of June, and the first eggs were taken at Lake Manitoba in 1894 on June 26. These dates seem late, since eggs were taken near Fort Anderson, Mackenzie, June 22, 1865, and downy young were found near Fort Yukon, Alaska, June 23, 1866.

Fall migration.—Unusually early arrivals have been noted on the Massachusetts coast by August 10; the average date when the first of the regular flight appear is September 6, and the greater flocks pass October 10–20; the first were seen near Baltimore, Md., September 12, 1894, and the same latitude in the interior seems to be reached a month later, as attested by the following dates of arrival: Heron Lake, Minn., October 11, 1886; Lincoln, Nebr., October 14, 1899; Denver, Colo., October 16, 1890; Longmont, Colo., October 20, 1901; Loveland, Colo., October 11, 1903. On the coast of California migrants arrive the last of August.

Oidemia perspicillata (Linn.).   Surf Scoter.

Breeding range.—This species breeds in northeastern Quebec (Point de Monts), southern Labrador, and Newfoundland, north as far as Hudson Strait; it is a summer visitor to the east coast of Greenland (Kangerajuk) and to the west coast as far north as Disco Bay, but is not known to breed; accidental in northern Europe; breeds abundantly at Fort Churchill, Hudson Bay, at Great Slave Lake, probably at Athabaska Lake, and north to the Arctic coast, west to the mouth of the Mackenzie. It is a common breeder on the headwaters of the Yukon, and from Sitka north to Kotzebue Sound. The species apparently is lacking on the north coast of Alaska, but nonbreeding birds are abundant on the coast of northeastern Siberia. Nonbreeders are found also all through the summer on the Atlantic coast south to Long Island and on the Pacific coast to Lower California.

Winter range.—The surf scoter remains around the Gulf of St. Lawrence until forced away by ice, and passes the winter from about the Bay of Fundy south to Florida. It is enormously abundant from Massachusetts to New Jersey, and still common to North Carolina; accidental in the Bermudas; it visits commonly the Great Lakes and extends south rarely to Louisiana (New Orleans, March 20, 1890), Illinois (opposite St. Louis, May 3, 1876), Kansas (Lawrence, October 29, 1887), Nebraska (Lincoln, October 7, 1896; Omaha), Colorado (Loveland, October 31, 1899; Denver, October 22, 1899), Wyoming (Douglas, October 19, 1893); on the Pacific coast from the Near Islands, and the Aleutians south to San Quentin Bay, Lower California.

Spring migration.—Birds from the south occasionally return to Nova Scotia late in March, more commonly the first week in April, and reach their breeding grounds about the first week in May. Those that migrate through the interior are nearly three weeks later. The Alaskan breeding grounds are reached about the middle of May. Eggs have been taken at Fort Anderson June 25 and downy young near Fort Yukon June 23.

Fall migration.—In 1900 stragglers appeared off the coasts of Maryland and Virginia the last week in August, about three weeks earlier than usual. The first fall migrants commonly arrive on the coast of Massachusetts and Long Island Sound the middle of September and are followed the second week in October by the main flight. The last leave the Gulf of St. Lawrence on the average November 7. Arrivals on the Great Lakes are rather later than in corresponding latitudes on the coast. A few surf scoters are seen on the California coast in July and August, though the main body hardly appears before November. They leave St. Michael, Alaska, and the upper Mackenzie about the middle of October.

Erismatura jamaicensis (Gmel.). Ruddy Duck.

Breeding range.—The principal summer home of the ruddy duck is in the upper Mississippi Valley and the contiguous portions of central Canada: it is rare east of the Alleghenies; breeds regularly from Maine to northern Ungava; rare visitant in Newfoundland; nesting rarely south to Massachusetts (Cape Cod) and probably in Rhode Island (Sakonnet); tolerably common in southern Ontario, Michigan, and Wisconsin, and probably breeds casually in Ohio and Illinois. West of the Mississippi it breeds regularly to southern Minnesota and northwestern Nebraska and rarely in Kansas. The breeding range then dips strongly to the south in the mountains through Colorado to northern New Mexico (La Jara and Stinking Spring lakes), central Arizona (Stoneman Lake, altitude 6,200 feet), southern California (Los Angeles County), northern Lower California to about latitude 31°, and probably northwestern Chihuahua (Pacheco). The breeding range on the Pacific slope extends north at least to central British Columbia (Cariboo District); in the interior to Great Slave Lake and Hudson Bay (York Factory). The above is the normal breeding range, but this species has the peculiar habit of establishing colonies far to the southward. Such colonies have been discovered at Santiago, near the southern end of Lower California, in the Valley of Mexico, at the Lake of Duenas, Guatemala, and on the islands of Cuba, Porto Rico, and Carriacou. The breeding season of these isolated colonies bears no relation to the usual breeding time in the bird's ordinary range. In northern North Dakota the earliest eggs are deposited the first week in June; in Manitoba and Saskatchewan incomplete sets were found the middle of June; the same date—the middle of June—marks the deposition of the eggs in central Colorado. The first half of June may be said to be the usual time for the beginning of nesting. On Cape Cod, Massachusetts, downy young were taken August 17; in northern New Mexico September 17; in southern Lower California, November 16; at Lake Duenas, Guatemala, in June; while in Cuba and Porto Rico eggs were taken in November, and on Carriacou Island in January.

Winter range.—In its choice of climate and environment the ruddy duck varies widely. While many individuals retire in winter to the southern part of the range, to southern Lower California, Tepic, Valley of Mexico, Oaxaca, and central Guatemala, others remain as far north as southern British Columbia. The northern limit in the Rocky Mountain region is Arizona and New Mexico; the species does not seem to remain through the winter in northern Texas, but at this season it is found in southern Illinois, Pennsylvania, the coast of Massachusetts, and even to Maine. During the winter the ruddy duck has been recorded in the Bermudas, the Bahamas (New Providence),

Jamaica, Martinique, Grenada, Barbados, and once in Central America—outside of Guatemala—at Irazu, Costa Rica. From the Chesapeake Bay to Florida it is quite a common winter resident, though it is being rapidly diminished in numbers.

Spring migration.—The ruddy duck is rather a late migrant. Throughout its winter district, northward movements occur late in March, and just north of this region it appears early in April. Average dates of arrival are: Erie, Pa., April 16; Oberlin, Ohio, April 15 (earliest April 7, 1903); Heron Lake, Minn., April 10 (earliest April 3, 1889); eastern Nebraska, April 7; Cheyenne, Wyo., April 21; southern Manitoba, May 5 (earliest, April 26, 1891). The first migrant was seen at Osler, Saskatchewan, May 7, 1893, and at Fort Keogh, Mont., April 21, 1889.

Fall migration.—An excellent series of observations at Alexandria, Va., extending over sixteen years, fixes September 30 as the average date of arrival on the Potomac (earliest, August 20, 1889). The average date when the species becomes common is October 25. On the Massachusetts coast the ruddy duck is most common in October and November. Farther west in the same latitude migration is somewhat earlier, and the northern States, from Pennsylvania to Minnesota, are deserted the first half of November. The first date of arrival at Barbados is September 13, 1887.

Nomonyx dominicus (Linn.). Masked Duck.

This is a tropical species that lives principally in the West Indies and in eastern South America. It is common in Argentina to the Rio Negro and north through eastern and central Brazil to Guiana, Venezuela, and the islands of Trinidad, Barbados, St. Croix, Porto Rico, Haiti, Jamaica, and Cuba. This may be considered the regular range. In western South America the masked duck has been noted at Concepcion, Chile, both in June and September, 1894—this is directly west of its center of abundance in Argentina—at Tatarenda, in eastern Bolivia, and Lake Titacaca, in the western part; at Sarayacu and the river Peripa, in Ecuador; twice in Panama, once in Guatemala, and four times in Mexico (Orizaba, Jalapa, Matamoras, Escuinapa). Just across the river from Matamoras, at Brownsville, Tex., is the only place in the United States where it has been found that it seemed to be at home. As it was noted July 22, 1891, it probably breeds there. Strays have been found in Vermont (Alburg Springs, September 26, 1857), Wisconsin (near Newville, November, 1870), Massachusetts (Malden, August 27, 1889), and Maryland (Elkton, September 8, 1905).

The species is not strictly nonmigratory, but the data are insufficient to allow of exact statements concerning its migration.

DISTRIBUTION AND MIGRATION OF GEESE.

Chen hyperborea (Pall.).   Lesser Snow Goose.

Breeding range.—Much remains to be learned of the boundaries of the summer home of the snow geese. "Vast numbers" of this goose were seen on the northwestern portion of Banks Land, latitude 74°, August 19, 1851, as though they had come from more northern breeding grounds, and in the spring of 1851 and 1852 flocks were seen passing north in the vicinity of the northern shores of this island; and yet no snow geese have been reported by any of the various expeditions that have summered on the islands immediately to the north of Banks Land. Snow geese are known to breed along the Arctic coast east of the Mackenzie River and to cross to Victoria Land, but here the record ends. Wollaston Land and Victoria Land form an enormous island whose interior has never been visited by white men. Many explorers have passed through the region to the northward, but no one has reported a snow goose in the whole district east of longitude 115° and north of latitude 70°, with the exception of a single flock seen near Bellot Strait in June, 1859, and three wanderers found in June, 1882, at Fort Conger, a thousand miles north of the regular range. Ross lived for three years at the base of the Boothia Peninsula without seeing a snow goose. Parry found but few birds and only one nest during his two years' sojourn on Melville Peninsula, and Kumlein reports them as rare visitants at Cumberland Sound. It follows, therefore, by exclusion, that the great bulk of the snow geese breed south of a line drawn from the north end of Southampton Island to the south end of Melville Island. It is supposed that the lesser snow goose is the form breeding at the mouth of the Mackenzie River, and east to about longitude 115°. It follows, therefore, that the greater snow goose is restricted in its breeding range to the district from Melville Peninsula to Victoria Land, an area perhaps half as large as Greenland, as yet scarcely visited by an ornithologist.

The most western breeding place of the lesser snow goose is Richards Island, on the eastern side of the mouth of the Mackenzie River; thence it ranges eastward to about Coronation Gulf. There seem to be two routes by which the snow geese reach their summer home. They are common in winter in California; indeed, this seems to be their principal winter abode. In the spring migration some continue up the coast to Alaska, but all observers agree that they are not common in Alaska during the spring migration. On the other hand, the species is an abundant migrant along the Mackenzie at Fort Simpson, just south of the breeding grounds, and the flocks in spring fly at a great height on their course toward the north. This is just the route the snow geese would take from California to their breeding grounds if they migrate by the most direct route. Though occurring accidentally in northern Europe and found on the Arctic coast of northeastern Asia, sometimes in considerable numbers, the lesser snow goose is not, as yet, known to breed in the Eastern Hemisphere.

Winter range.—Both forms of the snow goose occur during the winter season in the lower Mississippi Valley. It seems probable that in this district the Mississippi River is the approximate dividing line between the two forms, to the westward *C. hyperborea* being the more common, to the eastward, *C. nivalis.* Both forms winter as far north as southern Illinois, and the lesser snow goose is abundant in winter in Louisiana and Texas, and ranges south in Mexico to Guanajuato and Jalisco, and rarely to northern Lower California. It winters sparingly in southern Colorado, more commonly in Utah, abundantly in Nevada, and along the Pacific coast from southern California (Orange County) to southern British Columbia. On the Asiatic side it winters south to Japan.

Spring migration.—Writing many years ago, Ross states that the lesser snow goose arrives at Great Slave Lake earlier than the greater. Recent records of spring migration confirm this statement, and our present knowledge of isothermal lines affords a satisfactory explanation. It is considered that the common species in eastern North Dakota is *C. nivalis,* while the bird of Montana is *C. hyperborea.* Long-continued observations in the valley of the Red River of the North indicate that the first *C. nivalis* arrive on the average at latitude 47° on April 15; at the same latitude in central Montana the first migrants of *C. hyperborea* appear April 6. The more eastern birds advance to Aweme, Manitoba, latitude 50°, April 22, while at this latter date the van has reached Edmonton, Alberta, latitude 54°. Yet these more western and northern birds (lesser snow geese) are actually traveling in warmer weather than their eastern relations migrating at a later date; for during the last third of April the temperature at Edmonton averages about 2 degrees warmer than at Aweme.

Further advance of the lesser snow goose is recorded during the spring of 1904 to Fort Vermilion, latitude 58°, April 26, and to Fort Simpson, latitude 62°, May 2. East of Fort Simpson at Southampton Island, in Hudson Bay, this same spring the first snow geese were not seen until thirty-three days later—June 4—while to the westward, at Point Barrow, Alaska, more than 500 miles farther north, the first lesser snow geese arrive just about the same time as at Fort Simpson. The lesser snow geese that reach their breeding grounds by way of Alaska probably winter at least 800 miles farther north than those of the Mississippi Valley, and spring opens on the Pacific coast much earlier than in the interior.

The most northern records of the lesser snow goose are on Banks Land, where it arrived at Princess Royal Islands, latitude 73°, May 31,

1851, and at Mercy Bay, latitude 74°, May 31, 1852. The average rate of migration from central Montana, April 6, to Mercy Bay, May 31, is 33 miles per day.

During spring migration there is much difference in the length of time spent at different points of its route. In northern Texas the first appear March 4 and the last leave April 6, each being average dates; the extremes are February 18, 1887, and April 12, 1895; in other words, the snow goose is usually thirty-three days in passing northern Texas, and may linger fifty-four days. At the northern boundary of the United States, these periods are reduced about one-third, while still farther north near Lake Athabasca the species was present in 1901 for at least fourteen days, in 1903 for fifteen days, and at Fort Simpson in 1904 for twenty-three days. They arrive on the shore of Norton Sound, Alaska, from May 5 to 15, and at Nulato, on the Yukon, about May 9.

Fall migration.—Early migrants of the lesser snow goose were noted at Parry Bay, latitude 72°, August 13, 1821; at Point Barrow, latitude 70°, August 15, 1883; at Darnley Bay, latitude 69°, August 17, 1848; St. Michael, latitude 64°, September 2, 1878; Terry, Mont., latitude 47°, September 12, 1904; Stockton, Cal., latitude 38°, about September 29; central Texas, latitude 31°, about October 11. These dates indicate that the most northern breeders do not remain so long as ten weeks on the breeding grounds, and that they occupy fifty-eight days in retracing the path that required sixty-eight days during the spring migration.

The last seen on Banks Land were noted September 7, 1850; near Fort Norman, October 3, 1903; at mouth of the Yukon, about October 10; ten days later the last cross the boundary of the United States to the Mississippi watershed and desert central Nebraska about the first week in November.

Chen hyperborea nivalis (Forst.). Greater Snow Goose.

Breeding range.—The greater snow goose is enormously abundant on both the eastern and the western shores of Hudson Bay during spring migration, and these birds might be supposed to pass from these points approximately north to their breeding grounds. If such is the case it is somewhat strange that they have never been found breeding on any of the northern islands; nor have they been noted in migration anywhere north, northeast, or east of Hudson Bay, except the few seen at Igloolik, a few noted by Kumlein in Cumberland Bay, some stragglers that have wandered to the west coast of Greenland, and three birds seen by Greeley's party June 12–13, 1882, in Grinnell Land, latitude 82°. As already stated in connection with the lesser snow goose, it is probable that these Hudson Bay geese eventually turn to the northwestward and breed for the most part on Victoria Land.

Winter range.—During winter the greater snow goose has occurred in Cuba, Isle of Pines, Jamaica, and Porto Rico. Sometimes it has appeared in Cuba in quite large numbers. It is not usually common anywhere south of North Carolina. On this coast and as far as Chesapeake Bay it is not rare; a few are found in winter even as far north as Massachusetts. There is no sharply defined line in the Mississippi Valley between the winter ranges of the greater and the lesser forms. In general the greater snow goose is the more common east of the Mississippi River, and winters from southern Illinois to the Gulf.

Spring migration.—Throughout North America, north of Virginia and east of the immediate vicinity of Hudson Bay, the greater snow goose is a rare visitant; most of the spring dates in this region fall between March 20 and April 10. In the Mississippi Valley migration begins in February, and the first migrants appear north of the winter range early in March; the average date of arrival in central Iowa is March 22, and in northern Iowa March 26; southern Minnesota is reached April 6, southern Manitoba April 22, and in 1904 the first were noted in northern Hudson Bay June 4. The last leave the Gulf coast about the 1st of April; the average date for eleven years of the last seen at Aweme, Manitoba, is May 15, and the latest date May 20, 1903.

Fall migration.—One of the earliest dates of arrival of this species in New England is October 2, 1896, at Lake Umbagog; there are a few other October dates for New England. About the middle of October the earliest migrants appear on Chesapeake Bay, and the last of the month they arrive in Cuba and have been recorded in the Bermudas. In the fall the average date of arrival at Aweme, Manitoba, is September 28, and the earliest September 24, 1901; central Iowa is reached October 17, and the Gulf coast the last of the month. The average date of the last seen in the fall at Aweme, Manitoba, is October 20 (latest October 31, 1900).

Chen cærulescens (Linn.). Blue Goose.

Breeding range.—According to reports of Indians the blue goose nests in the interior of northern Ungava, but the nest and eggs are unknown to science, and there is no record of the presence of the birds anywhere in summer. During migration the species has been noted as an occasional visitant as far west as the western shore of Hudson Bay in the vicinity of Fort Churchill and east to New Hampshire.

Winter range.—The lower portion of the Mississippi Valley, principally west of the river, seems to be the winter home of this rather rare goose. It is not uncommon on the Gulf coast of Louisiana and Texas, and north to Nebraska and southern Illinois. It has occurred rarely or casually to the eastward in the Bahamas (Inagua), Cuba, Florida (Tortugas); North Carolina (near Fort Macon); Pennsylvania (near Pittsburg, 1887); New Jersey, New York (Shinnecock Bay, Long Island); Rhode Island (Newport, October 16, 1892); Massachusetts (Gloucester, October 20, 1876); New Hampshire (Lake Umbagog, October 2, 1896); Ohio (Oberlin, October 28, 1896; Columbus, October 28, 1876); Ontario (Ottawa, October 11, 1886; Gravenhurst, 1886). Apparently the only record west of the Rocky Mountains is that of two taken near Stockton, Cal., about February 1, 1892.

Spring migration.—Not many notes on the migration of this species are available. The few records indicate that the van moves across the central Mississippi Valley during the latter half of March and crosses to Manitoba the last of April or early May.

The blue goose seems to be exceptional in the selection of its migration route. The general trend of migration among waterfowl in North America is northwest and southeast. The blue goose apparently breeds entirely east of Hudson Bay and winters for the most part west of the Mississippi River, so that its spring migration flight is toward the northeast, across at least 20 degrees of longitude. At this season the large flocks pass north along the eastern side of James Bay, these flocks occasionally containing a few snow geese; while the enormous flocks of the latter that migrate north along the west side of James Bay are accompanied by a few blue geese.

Fall migration.—The above dates of occurrences outside of the normal range show that the fall migration is chiefly southward across the eastern United States and that it occurs in October.

Chen rossii (Cassin). Ross Snow Goose.

Breeding range.—The nest and eggs of this goose are still unknown, and there is no summer record of the species. The westernmost arctic locality known is Fort Anderson, and it ranges thence east to Hudson Bay. It is rare at each of these extremes, and the natural supposition is that the breeding grounds are to the north of the intervening district, that is, between the meridians of 100° and 120° west longitude. Observations on the birds of this region have been made by several observers, but they seem not to have distinguished this small white species from the larger snow goose.

Winter range.—The present known winter home of the Ross goose is California, where it occurs along the coast south to Orange County (Newport), and north to Stockton and the San Joaquin Valley. One was taken at Comox, British Columbia, January, 1894, but this occurrence was probably accidental. A pair was seen and one taken at Bustillos Lake, Chihuahua, also probably accidental.

Migration range.—The path of migration of this goose seems to be different from that of any other species. It is a fair presumption that the principal route coincides with the districts in which the species is most common. The greater number pass from the breeding grounds to Great Slave Lake and Lake Athabasca, continue south to central and western Montana, and then turn southwest, cross the Rocky Mountains, and pass to central and southern California.

Spring migration.—Records that are in close agreement indicate that the average date of arrival in spring at Great Falls, Mont., is April 7, and at Columbia Falls, Mont., April 8. The average date at which the last one was seen in central Montana is April 24. The birds were noted on the lower Athabasca River May 31, 1903, and one was taken May 25, 1865, at Fort Anderson, near the Arctic coast. The latest spring records are of its occurrence at Lake Athabasca, June 3, 1903, and at the base of Kent Peninsula, Arctic coast, June 2, 1902. The record of one taken near Camp Harney, Oreg., April 12, 1876, seems to be the only one for that State. A few have been taken in southern British Columbia at Shuswap Lake, Kuper Island, and the mouth of the Fraser River; one was taken at Fort Keogh, Mont., April 25, 1892.

Fall migration.—The returning flocks have been recorded at Great Slave Lake, September 1, 1893, at Columbia Falls, Mont., October 10, 1893, and at Newport, Cal., November 10, 1900. The average date of arrival at Columbia Falls, Mont., is October 15, and the latest date October 28, 1896. A straggler was taken at Winnipeg, Manitoba, September 20, 1902.

Anser albifrons (Gmel.).   White-fronted Goose.

The typical species inhabits Europe and Asia, and is reported as having been taken in May and September at Angmagsalik and Tasinsak in eastern Greenland.

Anser albifrons gambeli (Hartl.).   American White-fronted Goose.

Breeding range.—This goose breeds on the shore of the mainland from the mouth of the Yukon around the north side of Alaska and east to Lake Beechey on Back River; also coastwise for a few miles back in northern Mackenzie, and up the Yukon at least as far as Fort Yukon. The birds seen by Preble at Fort Wrigley, on the Mackenzie, July 23, 1904, may or may not have been breeding; a few nest on the coast of northeastern Asia in the vicinity of Bering Strait.

In giving the above range no mention is made of the birds that breed on the west coast of Greenland, where the species is not uncommon. It is evident from Labrador and Atlantic coast records that Greenland birds do not come to the southwest; hence they probably go to the southeast, and should be classed as European birds.

Winter range.—The white-fronted goose winters in the whole southern half of the United States and south to Cuba and northern Mexico.

Along the whole Atlantic slope it is rare; formerly, perhaps, it was not uncommon, but at present it is hardly more than an occasional winter visitant north to the coast of New Jersey, and an accidental migrant to New England, thence north to Labrador, where it has only once been recorded. It is not common in the interior east of the Mississippi River, and winters from the Gulf to southern Illinois and southern Ohio. The species is somewhat more common in migration along the eastern portion of the plains, wintering in southern Texas and more commonly in northern Mexico. The principal winter home is on the Pacific slope from Cape St. Lucas, Lower California, and Lake Chapala, Jalisco, to southern British Columbia. The few Asiatic birds winter on the coasts of China and Japan.

Spring migration.—The average date when the first migrants reach central Nebraska is March 9; Keokuk, Iowa, March 19; Aweme, Manitoba, April 18 (earliest April 6, 1905); Indian Head, Saskatchewan, April 22; Fort Vermillion, Alberta, April 27, 1904; Fort Resolution, Mackenzie, May 7, 1860; Fort Simpson, May 11, 1904; Fort Enterprise, May 17, 1821; Fort Anderson, May 16, 1864, May 17, 1865; Coronation Gulf, May 31, 1851.

On the Pacific slope migration is somewhat earlier; the first appear at St. Michael, Alaska, April 25 to May 10; at Nulato, May 6–10; Kowak River, May 10, 1899; Point Barrow, May 16, 1882, May 25, 1883. During the second half of April the last migrants leave the region south of Iowa and Nebraska; the average of the last seen at Aweme, Manitoba, for six years is May 11, and the latest May 17, 1898; the last leave California the first week in May. The first eggs were found near the mouth of the Yukon May 27, 1879; downy young were seen on the Kowak River June 24, 1899.

Fall migration.—Adults begin to leave the most northern breeding grounds by the middle of July, but so slow is the movement southward that on the average the first do not appear in southern Manitoba until September 26 (earliest September 7, 1902), and they reach the winter home, Louisiana to Texas, about the middle of October. At the same time the earliest of the fall migrants appear in central California, but the main flight does not arrive before November. The species has been noted at Stockton, Cal., as early as September 7. The last was noted at Point Barrow, Alaska, August 18, 1882; at the Kowak River, September 12, 1898; at St. Michael about October 7, and near Fort Wrigley, Mackenzie, October 9, 1903. The average date when the last are seen at Aweme, Manitoba, is October 13, and the latest was November 3, 1899.

Anser fabalis (Lath.). Bean Goose.

An Old World species of accidental occurrence (once) in northern Greenland.

Branta canadensis (Linn.).   Canada Goose.

Breeding range.—The principal summer home of the Canada goose is the interior of Canada, from Saskatchewan and Alberta north to the limit of trees.   Eastward it breeds commonly in the interior of Ungava and rarely on the coast as far north as Okak and Ungava Bay.   It is not a rare breeder in Newfoundland, and is fairly common on the islands of the Gulf of St. Lawrence and thence west through Quebec and northern Ontario to the southern end of James Bay.   Any occurrences south of this district must be considered accidental or casual, though it has been recorded as nesting at Lexington, Mass., April, 1888, and once at Hartland, Vt.

In the interior of North America the breeding range extends somewhat farther south.   A hundred years ago the species bred commonly in all the northern third of the Mississippi Valley and not uncommonly to the latitude of St. Louis.   Now the number of pairs breeding south of the latitude of central Iowa is very small, though even of late years the Canada goose has been known to breed at Samburg and at Reelfoot Lake, Tennessee, which seem to be the most southern localities known east of the Rocky Mountains.   A few breed in Kentucky, and the number increases slightly in Indiana and Illinois and the southern third of Michigan and Wisconsin.   North of this and throughout much of Minnesota the species is a regular and not uncommon summer resident.   The Canada goose formerly bred in Kansas; now it breeds rarely in Nebraska and southern South Dakota; regularly in North Dakota and northward.   The species still breeds in the northern third of Colorado, in northern Utah, northern Nevada, southern Oregon and northward.   A half century ago it was recorded as breeding as far south as southern New Mexico.   The western boundary of the breeding range extends from the interior of British Columbia to the upper Yukon and to Fort Yukon, with a few stragglers west to the Yukon mouth.

Winter range.—The principal winter home is the southern half of the Mississippi Valley west of the Mississippi River, but the species is not rare in the eastern United States from Florida to Maryland, occasionally to Massachusetts, and is recorded during the winter in Maine, Nova Scotia, Quebec, and even in Newfoundland.   The normal winter range in the interior extends to southern Indiana and southern Illinois, but a few have been noted in winter in Ohio, southern Ontario, southern Michigan, southern Wisconsin, Nebraska, southern Colorado, and southern Utah.   The winter home includes all of the Pacific coast region north to British Columbia, but in California typical *B. canadensis* inhabits the interior rather than the seashore.   The Canada goose is an accidental visitant to the Bermudas and to the West Indies (Jamaica and probably St. Croix).

Spring migration.—More records on the movements of the Canada goose have been contributed than on any other three waterfowl combined. A synopsis of the most important of these notes is presented, both for the purpose of indicating the time of the principal migration movements and also of calling attention to the wide differences in the records from contiguous localities in the case of a locally distributed species like the goose.

Dates of arrival in spring of the Canada goose.

ATLANTIC COAST.

Place.	Number of years' record.	Average date of spring arrival.	Earliest date of spring arrival.
Central Maryland	6	Mar. 22	Feb. 15, 1892
Berwyn, Pa	5	Mar. 5	Feb. 18, 1901
Renovo, Pa	3	Mar. 15	Mar. 12, 1899
Hares Valley, Pa	5	Mar. 12	Feb. 19, 1887
Central Pennsylvania	19	Mar. 17	Feb. 13, 1892
Erie, Pa	4	Mar. 21	Mar. 2, 1902
Central New Jersey	16	Mar. 22	Feb. 4, 1890
Oak Orchard Light, New York	9	Mar. 18	Mar. 4, 1890
Montauk Point, Long Island	8	Feb. 24	Feb. 15, 1893
Shelter Island, Long Island	8	Mar. 14	Mar. 10, 1892
Central New York	20	Mar. 13	Jan. 31, 1890
Plattsburg, N. Y		Mar. 22	Mar. 17, 1886
Jewett City, Conn	11	Mar. 19	Mar. 2, 1902
Central Connecticut	17	Mar. 17	Feb. 1, 1890
Block Island Light, Rhode Island	11	Mar. 16	Feb. 21, 1898
Framingham, Mass	8	Mar. 26	Mar. 20, 1887
Central Massachusetts	19	Mar. 17	Feb. 25, 1888
St. Johnsbury, Vt	3	Mar. 21	Mar. 13, 1902
Northern Vermont	6	Mar. 23	Mar. 13, 1902
Southern New Hampshire	13	Mar. 21	Mar. 11, 1892
Southern Maine	15	Mar. 24	Mar. 5. 1902
Plymouth, Me	9	Apr. 1	Mar. 23, 1880
Quebec City, Canada	12	Mar. 27	Mar. 1, 1894
Montreal, Canada	6	Mar. 22	Feb. 15, 1893
Godbout, Quebec	3	Apr. 8	Apr. 5, 1887
Grand Manan, New Brunswick	5	Mar. 22	Mar. 1, 1890
Chatham, New Brunswick	6	Mar. 19	Mar. 1, 1902
Scotch Lake, New Brunswick	5	Mar. 20	Mar. 14, 1902
Pictou, Nova Scotia	9	Mar. 7	Feb. 26, 1889
Halifax, Nova Scotia	5	Mar. 13	Feb. 23, 1892
North River, Prince Edward Island	4	Mar. 20	Mar. 9, 1888
Alberton, Prince Edward Island	8	Mar. 19	Mar. 10, 1889

MISSISSIPPI VALLEY.

Place.	Number of years' record.	Average date of spring arrival.	Earliest date of spring arrival.
Central Missouri	8	Feb. 11	(a)
Batavia, Ill	6	Feb. 22	Feb. 14, 1888
Chicago, Ill	18	Mar. 14	Jan. 15, 1897
Odin, Ill	5	Feb. 22	(a)
Lafayette, Ind	4	Mar. 2	Feb. 23, 1895
Bloomington, Ind	3	Mar. 5	Feb. 17, 1903
New Harmony, Ind	3	Feb. 8	Feb. 2, 1902
Frankfort, Ind	10	Feb. 19	Feb. 12, 1893
Waterloo, Ind	8	Mar. 14	Feb. 4, 1890
Sedan, Ind	6	Mar. 11	Feb. 13, 1891
Oberlin, Ohio	6	Mar. 9	Feb. 19, 1905
Wauseon, Ohio	4	Mar. 16	Feb. 23, 1888
Weymouth, Ohio	4	Mar. 13	Mar. 11, 1885
Petersburg, Mich	5	Mar. 5	Feb. 13, 1890
Battle Creek, Mich	5	Mar. 13	Mar. 8, 1903
Southern Michigan	19	Mar. 14	Feb. 23, 1890
Ottawa, Ontario	11	Apr. 4	Mar. 20, 1903
Southern Ontario	10	Mar. 16	Feb. 24, 1901
Southern Iowa	16	Mar. 1	Feb. 4, 1890
Storm Lake, Iowa	4	Feb. 17	Feb. 2, 1888
Spirit Lake, Iowa	7	Mar. 1	Feb. 23, 1886
Delavan, Wis	3	Mar. 4	Feb. 28, 1895
Southern Wisconsin	18	Mar. 13	Feb. 27, 1894
Heron Lake, Minn	4	Mar. 18	Feb. 23, 1886
Lanesboro, Minn	3	Mar. 21	Mar. 15, 1889
St. Paul, Minn	3	Mar. 22	Mar. 5, 1889
Elk River, Minn	4	Mar. 27	Mar. 11, 1885
Onaga, Kans	7	Feb. 14	(a)

a A few winter.

Dates of arrival in spring of the Canada goose—Continued.

MISSISSIPPI VALLEY—Continued.

Place.	Number of years' record.	Average date of spring arrival.	Earliest date of spring arrival.
Central Kansas	4	Feb. 13	(a)
Southern Nebraska	6	Feb. 21	(a)
Omaha, Nebr	4	Feb. 26	Feb. 12, 1898
Huron, S. Dak., and vicinity	6	Mar. 17	Mar. 2, 1889
Grand View, S. Dak., and vicinity	5	Feb. 23	Jan. 27, 1891
Argusville, N. Dak	6	Mar. 23	Mar. 8, 1892
Larimore, N. Dak	8	Mar. 21	Mar. 16, 1894
Aweme, Manitoba	11	Mar. 29	Mar. 9, 1905
Reaburn, Manitoba	9	Apr. 2	Mar. 25, 1900
Qu'Appelle, Saskatchewan	3	....do...	Mar. 25, 1905
Bulyea, Saskatchewan	....	....	Apr. 10, 1904
Indian Head, Saskatchewan	2	Apr. 1	Feb. 24, 1905
Fort Vermillion, Alberta	....	....	Apr. 15, 1904
Reindeer Lake, Saskatchewan	16	Apr. 30	Apr. 17, 1889
Fort Simpson, Mackenzie	14	Apr. 28	Apr. 22, 1904
Rathdrum, Idaho	2	Feb. 24	Feb. 3, 1901
Great Falls, Mont	3	Mar. 12	Mar. 10, 1889
Columbia Falls, Mont	5	Mar. 24	Mar. 17, 1895
Terry, Mont	10	Mar. 27	Feb. 28, 1892

a A few winter.

Dates of departure in spring of the Canada goose.

Place.	Number of years' record.	Average date of last one seen.	Latest date of last one seen.
Central West Virginia	3	Apr. 1	Apr. 21, 1886
Central Maryland	5	Apr. 4	Apr. 22, 1890
Berwyn, Pa	4	Apr. 11	Apr. 24, 1898
Renovo, Pa	3	Apr. 15	Apr. 16, 1900
Central Pennsylvania	10	Apr. 9	May 5, 1894
Central New Jersey	6	Apr. 16	May 9, 1887
Oak Orchard Light, New York	....	....	May 14, 1890
Montauk Point Light, Long Island	11	Apr. 22	Apr. 29, 1890
Southern Mississippi	4	Mar. 26	Apr. 20, 1903
Keokuk, Iowa	6	Apr. 3	Apr. 23, 1893
Grapevine, Tex	11	Apr. 4	Apr. 15, 1899
Northern Texas	7	Apr. 4	Apr. 9, 1885

Spring arrival of the Canada goose.

Year.	Central Missouri.	Frankfort, Ind.	Southern Iowa.	Chicago, Ill.	Southern Wisconsin.	Southern Michigan.
1884	Feb. 1	....	....	Mar. 15	Mar. 16	Mar. 15
1885	....	....	Mar. 2	Mar. 29	Mar. 28	Mar. 27
1886	Feb. 10	....	Feb. 23	Mar. 17	Mar. 16	Mar. 12
1887	....	....	Feb. 28	Mar. 12	Mar. 6	Mar. 8
1888	....	....	Mar. 1	Mar. 18	Mar. 15	Mar. 14
1889	Feb. 11	Feb. 15	Mar 2	Mar. 7	Mar. 15	Mar. 18
1890	....	....	Feb. 26	....	Mar. 19	Mar. 7
1891	....	....	....	Mar. 2	....	Mar. 10
1892	....	....	Feb. 26	....	Mar. 4	Mar. 5
1893	Feb. 4	Feb. 12	Feb. 26	Mar. 12	Mar. 10	Mar. 5
1894	....	Feb. 14	Mar. 1	Mar. 9	Mar. 3	Mar. 16
1895	....	Feb. 25	....	Mar. 13	Mar. 12	Mar. 25
1896	....	Feb. 21	Feb. 25	Mar. 6	Mar. 8	....
1897	....	Feb. 14	....	Mar. 16	Mar. 19	Mar. 8
1898	....	Feb. 17	Mar. 5	Mar. 10	Mar. 9	....
1899	....	Feb. 20	....	Mar. 21	....	....
1900	....	Feb. 21	Feb. 28	Mar. 13	....	Mar. 26
1901	....	Feb. 27	....	Mar. 16	....	Mar. 27
1902	Feb. 11	....	Feb. 28	Mar. 19	Mar. 9	Mar. 14
1903	Feb. 10	....	Mar. 1	Mar. 13	Mar. 17	Mar. 8
1904	Feb. 20	....	Feb. 29	....	Mar. 13	Mar. 8
1905	Feb. 22	....	Feb. 26	....	Mar. 18	Mar. 11
Average	Feb. 11	Feb. 19	Mar. 1	Mar. 14	Mar. 13	Mar. 14

Spring arrival of the Canada goose—Continued.

Year.	Southern Ontario.	Ottawa, Ontario.	Lari-more, N. Dak.	Aweme, Manitoba.	Reaburn, Manitoba.	Terry, Mont.
1884	Mar. 13			Apr. 1		
1885	Mar. 25		Apr. 3			
1886			Mar. 22			
1887						
1888	Mar. 19					
1889	Mar. 12		Mar. 16			
1890	Mar. 12	Mar. 28	Mar. 24	Mar. 20		Mar. 27
1891						
1892						
1893		Apr. 8				Apr. 2
1894		Apr. 12	Mar. 16		Apr. 7	Mar. 18
1895	Mar. 26	Apr. 12	Mar. 22			
1896		Apr. 10		Mar. 26	Mar. 28	Mar. 27
1897	Mar. 12	Mar. 31		Apr. 7	Apr. 8	Apr. 4
1898	Mar. 14	Mar. 29		Apr. 7	Apr. 7	Apr. 3
1899		Apr. 8		Apr. 9	Apr. 10	
1900	Mar. 13	Apr. 5		Mar. 23	Mar. 25	Mar. 25
1901				Mar. 28	Apr. 2	
1902				Mar. 14	Mar. 27	
1903				Mar. 28	Mar. 27	Apr. 1
1904		Mar. 26	Mar. 24	Mar. 30		Mar. 22
1905	Mar. 19	Mar. 31	Mar. 24			Mar. 20
Average	Mar. 16	Apr. 4	Mar. 21	Mar. 29	Apr. 2	Mar. 27

The Canada goose is about the earliest water bird to migrate in spring, and throughout the whole course of its journey from its winter home to the Arctic coast it keeps close to the melting ice and the opening streams. The following dates seem a fair average for the time of arrival in the several districts:

Locality.	Latitude.		Date.
	°	′	
Southeastern Iowa	40	30	Feb. 20
Southern Minnesota	44	00	Mar. 19
Central Minnesota	46	00	Mar. 28
Southern Manitoba	50	00	Apr. 6
Alberta	58	00	Apr. 22
Southern Mackenzie	62	00	May 3
Northern Mackenzie	66	00	May 12

If the time occupied in passing from one district to the next is compared with the distance traveled, it will be found that the speed varies widely in different parts of the migration route. The following are approximate averages:

From latitude 40° to latitude 44°, 9 miles per day.
From latitude 44° to latitude 46°, 15 miles per day.
From latitude 46° to latitude 50°, 20 miles per day.
From latitude 50° to latitude 58°, 23 miles per day.
From latitude 58° to latitude 62°, 25 miles per day.
From latitude 62° to latitude 66°, 30 miles per day.

A great many records of the spring arrival of the Canada goose at the posts of the Hudson's Bay Company are available. Since this bird forms an important part of the food, both of the Indians and of the company's employees, a record is kept of its arrival each spring, and a reward is given to the person that secures the first one. These records show that the Canada goose is among the most variable of birds in the time of its arrival. This is natural, since its migration seems to depend almost wholly upon the presence of open water, and this varies much with the seasons. The record at Fort Simpson covers thirteen years between 1881 and 1894, and the average date of arrival is April 28, with extremes of fifteen days from April 23 to May 8. The average variation—the "probable error"—in time of arrival is 4.1 days, i. e., if the Canada goose is noted as arriving on a certain date in any one year at that latitude the probability is that this date is within 4.1 days of the average date of arrival at that locality. At Lac du Brochet Post, on Reindeer Lake, Saskatchewan, the following are the dates when the first Canada goose was seen:

1874..............May 5	1880..............May 5	1886..............Apr. 23
1875..............May 11	1881..............May 4	1887..............May 3
1876..............May 8	1882..............May 3	1888..............May 7
1877..............Apr. 27	1883..............Apr. 25	1889..............Apr. 17
1878..............Apr. 19	1884..............May 3	
1879..............Apr. 24	1885..............Apr. 29	

The average date of arrival is April 30, with extremes of twenty-four days from April 17 to May 11. The average variation is 5.9 days.

Eggs have been found in northern Indiana, southern Minnesota, and central Wyoming the first week in May, and sometimes even in April, and at Malheur Lake, Oregon, April 24. An early set was found May 4 near the Saskatchewan, and one May 11 near the Red Deer River, Alberta, but usually nesting in this district begins about the middle of May, and at the northern limit of the range not much before the middle of June.

Dates of arrival in the fall of the Canada goose.

Place.	Number of years' record.	Average date of first one seen.	Earliest date of first one seen.
Prince Edward Island.............................	8	Aug. 28	Aug. 22, 1889
Scotch Lake, New Brunswick.......................	3	Oct. 23	Oct. 21, 1902
Central Massachusetts.............................	5	Oct. 11	Sept. 4, 1889
Block Island, Rhode Island.......................	7	Oct. 21	Sept. 27, 1898
Montauk Point, Long Island.......................	9	Oct. 20	Sept. 30, 1888
Renovo, Pa.......................................	4	Oct. 24	Oct. 7, 1904
Central Pennsylvania.............................	8	Oct. 22	Oct. 15, 1894
Central New Jersey...............................	14	Oct. 18	Sept. 23, 1897
Alexandria, Va...................................	16	Oct. 20	Oct. 5, 1888
Atlantic, N. C...................................	......	......	Oct. 20, 1899
Anderson, S. C...................................	......	......	Oct. 10, 1902
Chipley, Fla.....................................	......	......	Oct. 8, 1902
Aweme, Manitoba..................................	6	Aug. 14	Aug. 3, 1901
Central South Dakota.............................	3	Sept. 23	Aug. 20, 1890
Northern Nebraska................................	7	Oct. 7	Sept. 7, 1888
Onaga, Kans......................................	4	Oct. 18	Oct. 3, 1891
Grapevine, Tex...................................	9	Oct. 9	Sept. 30, 1904
Central Wisconsin................................	8	Oct. 12	Sept. 30, 1892
Central Iowa.....................................	7	Oct. 14	Sept. 16, 1899
Keokuk, Iowa.....................................	8	Oct. 8	Sept. 27, 1895
Wauseon, Ohio....................................	4	Oct. 20	Oct. 10, 1887
Central Indiana..................................	5	Oct. 19	Oct. 6, 1902
Northern Illinois................................	4	Oct. 13	Sept. 28, 1895
Central Missouri.................................	4	Oct. 4	Sept. 23, 1900
Helena, Ark......................................	3	Oct. 4	Sept. 26, 1896
Southern Mississippi.............................	2	Nov. 12	Nov. 5, 1902

Dates of departure in the fall of the Canada goose.

Place.	No. of years' record.	Average date of last one seen.	Latest date of last one seen.
Columbia Falls, Mont	4	Nov. 20	Nov. 24, 1895
Aweme, Manitoba	6	Nov. 17	Dec. 2, 1899
Southern Ontario	4	Nov. 7	Nov. 10, 1901
Southern Michigan	4	Nov. 8	Nov. 25, 1890
Central Minnesota	8	Nov. 9	Dec. 1, 1890
Central Iowa	13	Nov. 18	Dec. 26, 1904
Keokuk, Iowa	7	Nov. 10	Dec. 4, 1900
Central Nebraska	4	Nov. 27	(a)
Prince Edward Island	6	Dec. 1	Dec. 22, 1889
Grand Manan, New Brunswick	4	Nov. 15	Nov. 20, 1890
Montreal, Canada	4	Nov. 4	Nov. 14, 1896
Southern Massachusetts	8	Nov. 18	Dec. 28, 1877
Mantauk Point, Long Island	8	Nov. 21	Dec. 19, 1889
Renovo, Pa	6	Nov. 9	Nov. 18, 1903
Central Pennsylvania	7	Nov. 14	Dec. 6, 1899
Berwyn, Pa	6	Nov. 16	Dec. 15, 1891
Central New Jersey	9	Nov. 19	Dec. 10, 1902

a A few winter.

Branta canadensis hutchinsii (Rich.). Hutchins Goose.

Breeding range.—This is the most northern of the several forms of Canada goose and nests from Melville Peninsula north to latitude 70° and west along the shores and islands of the Arctic coast to the mouth of the Mackenzie and through the interior of Alaska to the Kowak River. Apparently it does not breed in the interior of North America south of the Barren Grounds, but on the Pacific coast it breeds in the valley of the Kowak River and south to the mouth of the Knik River; also abundantly in the western Aleutians and on the Near Islands. One was taken June 10 at Kingwah Fjord and a few have been taken at Disco and Godhaven, Greenland, but there seems to be no breeding record east of Hudson Bay.

Winter range.—The Hutchins goose seems to be more common in California during the winter season than elsewhere, though it is not rare in the rest of the southern United States west of the Mississippi River. Its normal eastern range is to Hudson Bay, Illinois, and Louisiana. It is known as a rare migrant in Maine and a century ago seems to have been not uncommon on the New England coast. A few pass through western New York, Ontario, and Ohio, and less rarely through Indiana. Southern Wisconsin seems to be the farthest north that it has been recorded in the interior during the winter season. It appears to be unknown on the Atlantic coast south of Virginia, but on the Pacific it passes south to San Rafael, Lower California, and probably to Lake Chapala, Jalisco, and winters north to southern British Columbia. One specimen is recorded from the city of Vera Cruz, Mexico, where it was accidental.

Spring migration.—Records are insufficient to allow of exact statements in regard to the movements of the Hutchins goose. In general it can be said that it migrates later than *B. canadensis*. The average date of its arrival in northern North Dakota and southern Manitoba is April 12, fully two weeks later than the Canada goose arrives. Hudson Bay is reached early in May and the extreme northern part of the range not much before the first of June. The first was noted near the mouth of the Yukon River May 8 and on the Kowak River May 14. Eggs were taken near Fort Anderson, Mackenzie, June 10, 1864, and June 14, 1865.

Fall migration.—Small family parties begin to flock early in August and flocks appear at Aweme, Manitoba, on the average September 21 (earliest September 13, 1904). First arrivals were noted at Terry, Mont., September 22, 1904; Delavan, Wis., October 12, 1894; central Kansas, October 5–13; central California about the first of October. The last noted at Cape McDonnel, Great Bear Lake, was on September 25; at Fort Wrigley, Mackenzie, October 12, and on the Kowak River, Alaska, September 14.

Branta canadensis occidentalis (Baird). White-Cheeked Goose.

This form is confined to the Pacific slope and breeds from the Klamath Lakes and Lake Tahoe, north to Sitka and Mitkof Island. It winters from Washington south to San Diego County, Cal. It appears south of its breeding range in early November and starts north so early in the spring that after the middle of March few are left in the southern part of the winter range.

Branta canadensis minima Ridgw. Cackling Goose.

This form is confined during the breeding season to Alaska, where it breeds abundantly along the coast from the Kowak River to the north side of the Alaska Peninsula. It breeds very abundantly also on the western Aleutians. It winters in southern British Columbia and thence south to San Diego County, Cal. It has been known to wander east to Hudson Bay, Wisconsin, and Colorado.

It is the earliest goose to reach the mouth of the Yukon in spring migration, arriving there from the 25th to the 30th of April, a few days after the last have deserted the southern portion of the winter range. The return movement begins late in August, is at its height by the middle of September, and the first arrive in central California about the first of October. The species deserts the Yukon region the last of September or early in October, and the Aleutians about the middle of November.

Branta bernicla (Linn.). Brant.

This is the Old World species that breeds north of the mainland of Europe and extends west to the east coast of Greenland; winters in northern Europe, rarely south to the Mediterranean.

Branta bernicla glaucogastra (Brehm). White-bellied Brant.

Breeding range.—There is a lack of knowledge as to the dividing line between this form and the black brant (*B. nigricans*). It is known that the latter breeds on the Arctic coast of America east about to longitude 125° (Franklin Bay), and that the species reaches its summer home by migration from the west and southwest, and not from the south by way of the Mackenzie Valley. It is known that the eastern brant occurs in migration on Melville Peninsula and passes along the east coast of Boothia Peninsula, longitude 92°. There seems to be no record of brant on the Arctic coast of the mainland between Franklin Bay and Boothia Peninsula—nearly a thousand miles—and yet brant of some form are common on all the islands that lie between these two longitudes north of 74° latitude. It is practically certain that the brant swarming in Wellington Channel, directly north of Boothia Peninsula, are the eastern form. Brant were seen on September 7, 1850, at the south end of Banks Land, and as they were then in full tide of fall migration they were undoubtedly on their way to the Arctic coast of the mainland and belonged to the western form. A year later, August 19, 1851, "vast numbers" were seen in the northwestern part of the same island as they were gathering for their migration. These also, then, were probably the western form, and they bred commonly along the northern shore of this island. Melville Island is only 50 miles from Banks Land, and hence it is probable that the "brent geese" taken by Parry on this latter island were the black brant. The dates of migration are of no help in settling this question. Brant arrived on Melville Island June 6, 1820, before June 9, 1853, and were seen on the north coast of Banks Land soon after June 1, 1852, or at about the same date they arrived in 1882–3, at Point Barrow, considerably farther south. They were noted in the vicinity of Wellington Channel, about latitude 75°, June 3, 1851, June 2, 1853, and about June 9, 1854. Almost directly south the first were not noted on Boothia Peninsula, latitude 70°, until June 12, 1830; June 20, 1831; and June 8, 1859; and still farther south on Melville Peninsula not until June 14, 1822, and June 14, 1823. While on the west coast of Greenland, at latitude 72°, the first were seen May 29, 1850, and at the extreme northern limit of the range, above latitude 82°, near the northwestern part of Greenland, they arrived June 9, 1876; June 3, 1882; June 5, 1883.

The eastern brant breeds on the west coast of Greenland from Frederikshaab, latitude 62°, northward probably as far as land extends, certainly as far north as the north shore of Grinnell Land, latitude 82° 33'. It probably breeds also on the islands north of latitude 74° and west to Wellington Channel. Breeding records south of this district are unsatisfactory, though the species will probably be found to breed rarely on North Somerset Island.

Winter range.—It is common during the winter along the Atlantic coast from Florida to New Jersey, less common on Long Island, and rare during the winter in Rhode Island and Massachusetts. A straggler was secured on Barbados, November 15, 1876.

Records for the interior of North America are not numerous. Specimens are recorded from the Whitewater Valley, Indiana; Ottawa, Ontario, fall of 1887; Racine, Wis.; Omaha, Nebr., November 9, 1895; Lake Manitoba, spring of 1889; Fort Lyon, Colo., April 11, 1883; Comox, British Columbia, January 10, 1904.

Spring migration.—Since no brant in spring pass north along the west coast of Hudson Bay, all the individuals of the species must perform their spring migration on the Atlantic coast. They return in February to Long Island Sound, where they stay in mild winters, and appear on the southeastern coast of Massachusetts on the average February 23. They are common in these waters for six weeks. By the end of March the van has already reached northern Nova Scotia. They spend the next month around the Gulf of St. Lawrence, and then move slowly northward. All observers agree that the brant do not go around the east shore of Newfoundland, but steer more directly north across the Labrador Peninsula. The average date on which they reach latitude 46° in the Gulf of St. Lawrence is March 23, and it is not until May 30 that early arrivals have been recorded in latitude 79°, showing an average speed of 34 miles per day. The average date of arrival in latitude 82° is June 7, or an average speed from latitude 41° to latitude 82° of 28 miles per day. The most northern record of the brant is latitude 82° 33' on the north coast of Grinnell Land. Here it arrived June 9, 1876, and the first eggs were found June 21. A hundred miles to the south, at Ross Inlet, eggs were taken June 16, and at Cape Sabine, latitude 78° 40', June 17, 1900.

The last disappear from North Carolina waters the first week in April; most leave Cape Cod, Massachusetts, by April 24, and the remainder about the 1st of May, though at various times birds have been seen the last week of this month. The south shore of the Gulf of St. Lawrence is deserted usually June 9–12, just as the earliest brant are arriving on their breeding grounds.

Fall migration.—Southward-moving flocks of brant were seen August 20, 1876, at Cape Lieber, latitude 81° 30', ten weeks after the first had passed north. In less than three weeks the last had disappeared, i. e., they were not over three months on the breeding grounds. The black brant breeding at Point Barrow, Alaska, were present from June 5 to September 20, 1898, fifteen weeks, and this latter period is about as long as the interval spent at their breeding grounds by those small land birds of the Gulf States that migrate earliest in the fall.

Brant reappear in the Gulf of St. Lawrence late in September, and arrive at Long Island about the middle of October. They occupy less than sixty days in retracing their flight over the course to cover which in spring requires more than one hundred days. In the fall migration great numbers pass south along the west shore of Hudson Bay, but as the species is almost unknown in Manitoba and Ontario, these birds must pass through northern Quebec to gain the Atlantic coast.

Branta nigricans (Lawr.). Black Brant.

Breeding range.—The principal known breeding ground of this species is along the Arctic coast and islands in the vicinity of the mouth of the Anderson River. Thence westward a smaller number breed at Point Barrow. The species is common on the Siberian coast of the Chukchi Peninsula and west to the New Siberian Islands. As stated under the preceding species, it is probable that the brant breeding abundantly on Banks Land and in smaller numbers on Melville Island belong to this species.

Winter range.—The main body of the black brant winters on the coast of California, especially at Bodega Bay and Tomales Bay. A few pass as far south as San Quentin Bay and Cerros Island, Lower California, and the species is known in winter north to the Straits of Juan de Fuca. It penetrates inland to Pyramid and Washoe lakes, Nevada; Malheur and Klamath lakes, Oregon, and on the Atlantic coast has straggled to Chatham, Mass.; Oneida Lake, New York; Islip and Great South Bay, Long Island, and Long Beach, New Jersey. On the Asiatic side the brant goes south in winter to Japan.

Spring migration.—Brant begin to move northward in early March, but proceed so slowly that it is the middle of May when they arrive at the mouth of the Yukon, and the last of May when they reach Kotzebue Sound; the dates of arrival at Point Barrow are June 13, 1882, June 7, 1883, and June 5, 1898; downy young were taken there July 10, 1898. Most of the birds have left the California coast by the last of April, and it is a little strange that one of the latest records south of Alaska should come from Lower California, where several brant were seen May 9 and 10 in San Quentin Bay.

Instead of taking the long course around the northwest coast of Alaska, some brant that nest near the mouth of the Mackenzie make a short cut across the interior of Alaska, and the species is abundant for a few days each spring at Fort Yukon and La Pierre House on its way north and is seen each spring at Fort McPherson passing north along Peel River.

Fall migration.—Migrants return to the mouth of the Yukon from the middle to the latter part of September, appear in British Columbia a month later, and reach the California coast in November. The latest dates for Point Barrow are September 21, 1882, and September 20, 1898.

Branta leucopsis (Bechst.). Barnacle Goose.

This species inhabits the northern parts of the Old World, and in migration reaches Greenland, where it has been taken repeatedly on the eastern coast around Scoresby Sound, and a few times on the western side at Julianshaab and Fiskernœs.

The barnacle goose has been taken several times in the United States, and though some of these birds may have escaped from captivity, it is not probable that all are escapes. The species is recorded as taken at Currituck Sound, North Carolina, October 31, 1870; near Jamaica Bay, Long Island, about October 20, 1876; North Chatham, Mass., November 1, 1885; Marshfield, Vt.; Montreal, Canada; Okak, Labrador; Racine, Wis., December, 1850; and one at James Bay, near Rupert House.

Philacte canagica (Sevast.). Emperor Goose.

Breeding range.—This is an Arctic species, with a very restricted range in the vicinity of Bering Sea. It breeds along the Alaskan coast from the mouth of the Kuskokwim River north to Cape Espenberg and the southern shore of Kotzebue Sound. The principal breeding ground is near the mouth of the Yukon River, but a few pass west to St. Lawrence Island and to the Asiatic coast, and breed on the Chukchi Peninsula in the vicinity of East Cape.

Winter range.—The Aleutian chain is the main winter home of the species, outside of which a few are found west to the Near and the Commander Islands and east to Bristol Bay and Sitka. Stragglers wander south and have been taken twice on Vancouver Island and three times in California—Eureka, winter of 1884; Gridley, November 1, 1895; San Francisco market, October 8, 1900. Four were taken and a dozen or more noted, evidently members of a straggling flock, December 12, 1902, in the Hawaiian Islands.

Spring migration.—At the extreme southwestern part of the range the northward movement begins late in March. The latter part of April the emperor goose moves from the southern to the northern shores of the Aleutian Islands and remains there for several weeks. As soon as the melting snows expose mud flats on the coast of Norton Sound the birds make the ocean flight to their breeding grounds, where they arrive from May 15 to 25. Eggs have been taken June 5, and young birds late in June.

Fall migration.—The geese regain their feathers after the summer molt about the middle of August, and a few at once start south. The earliest date on the Aleutians is August 31. Most of the species remain at the breeding grounds until October and then are forced slowly south by the approach of winter, scarcely reaching the southwestern limit of the usual winter range before early December.

Dendrocygna autumnalis (Linn.). Black-bellied Tree-duck.

This tree duck comes into the United States in the lower Rio Grande Valley and breeds as far north as Corpus Christi; it arrives in April, the bulk leave in September and the last in November. It ranges throughout most of Middle America from western Mexico (Mazatlan) to Panama (River Truando); accidental in Jamaica. It winters in Mexico at least as far north as central Vera Cruz (Vega del Casadero) and Mazatlan. North of this district it is strictly migratory, and throughout most, if not all, of its range in Central America there seems to be a shifting of location between the winter and the summer homes, but no data are available to determine the movements with accuracy.

Dendrocygna fulva (Gmel.). Fulvous Tree-duck.

Resident in southern Louisiana (Lake Catharine, The Rigolets, New Orleans) and from Mexico north to central Texas (Galveston, North Concho River), southern Arizona (Fort Whipple), central California, and west central Nevada (Lake Washoe). In California the species has been found breeding north to Los Banos in the San Joaquin Valley, has been taken in winter in the Sacramento Valley (Marysville), and has been noted probably as a straggler in Marin County (Inverness). The breeding range in Mexico is from Lake Chapala, Lake Cuitzeo, and the Valley of Mexico northward, while in winter the species passes south to Guerrero and Chiapas. It has occurred in Lower California.

An unusual case of wandering occurred in the fall of 1905. A flock of ten was seen at Grays Harbor, Washington, on October 3, and one was secured. A straggler was taken at Swan Island, North Carolina, in July, 1886.

The migration habits of the fulvous tree-duck are peculiar; one of the most northern records (Marysville, Cal.) is of a winter specimen, and almost the most southern (Lake Cuitzeo, Mexico) is of breeding birds. While the species as a whole moves north to breed and south to winter—these movements occurring in April and October—a few remain throughout the year in most of the range.

The same species is found in South America, where it breeds commonly in the vicinity of Buenos Aires, and occurs thence north through Uruguay and Rio Grande do Sul, Brazil, to central Paraguay (Asuncion) and northern Argentina (Tucuman, Fortin Donovan). Accidentals have been noted in central Chile (Paine), northern Peru (Moyobamba), northwestern Ecuador (Vinces), and east central Brazil (Port Capuno, Rio Belmonte). Questionable records appear from Venezuela and the Island of Trinidad.

The migration habits of the fulvous tree-duck in South America are the same as in North America; a few are resident at either extreme of the range, while the bulk move south to central Argentina to breed, and retire to northern Argentina to spend the colder portion of the year. The greater part of the species is, therefore, confined to the immediate vicinity of the Rio de La Plata and the lower valleys of its larger branches in a district approximately 700 miles in length north and south, and scarcely half that in width. This same species is found also in southern Africa and southern Asia.

[Dendrocygna viduata (Linn.).   White-faced Tree-duck.

This species does not come north to the United States, but has occurred as a straggler in Cuba (three records) and in Barbados (one flock). Its regular range is from Central Colombia and northeastern South America to Peru, Bolivia, and Paraguay; less common in Argentina, south to Buenos Aires. It seems to perform no regular migration in any part of its range.

The same species, or one so closely allied that it has not yet been separated, inhabits much of Africa from ocean tô ocean, and from about 15° north latitude (Senegal) to 27° south latitude (Potchefstroom); also the island of Madagascar. Its range in Africa, therefore, is more extensive than in South America, and on the whole is in about the same latitude, for the range in South America extends from latitude 11° N. to latitude 34° S.]

[Dendrocygna arborea (Linn.).   Whistling Duck.

This duck is known only from the West Indies, where it ranges from Andros Island, Bahamas, through all the Greater Antilles to St. Croix, Virgin Gorda, and Barbados of the Lesser Antilles; said to be a migrant, but the available data do not suffice to trace its movements.]

[Dendrocygna discolor (Scl. & Salv.).   Southern Red-billed Tree-duck.

This duck ranges north to the island of Trinidad and to Davila, Panama. It is of wide distribution in northern South America from Colombia to Guiana and south to eastern Peru and northern Brazil. It appears to be resident throughout its range, unless possibly in the extreme northern part, Trinidad, and Panama.]

DISTRIBUTION AND MIGRATION OF SWANS.

Olor cygnus (Linn.).   Whooping Swan.

This swan is common in Europe and Asia, and formerly was not rare in Greenland, where it is now nearly exterminated. Single specimens of late years have been taken at Atangmik, Godthaab, Ivigtut, and Arsuk in southern Greenland.

Olor columbianus (Ord).   Whistling Swan.

Breeding range.—The whistling swan breeds principally north of the Arctic Circle, but a few nest on Southampton and Nottingham islands in Hudson Bay, and the species is reported as breeding at Kennedy Lake in Baffin Land. It is fairly common during the breeding season along the Arctic coast in the vicinity of the mouth of the Mackenzie, and not rare throughout much of Alaska. A few pass to the islands of the Arctic Sea, even to latitude 74°. One of the parties of the

Biological Survey found the whistling swan breeding at Becharof Lake in southern Alaska, latitude 58°, this being the most southern breeding record. Thence it breeds along the Yukon, about Kotzebue Sound, and probably to Point Barrow. Though found on the Asiatic side at Bering Island, as yet there is no record of its breeding in that country. Accidental once in Scotland and once in the Bermudas.

Winter range.—Probably about as common on Chesapeake Bay during the winter as in any part of its winter home; many pass to the coast of North Carolina and a few to Florida. It winters regularly north to New Jersey, and during the winter of 1877–78, one remained on Nantucket Island, Massachusetts, in which State the species was common when the first settlers arrived, but is now so rare that it seems to have been recorded only four times in the last thirty years. It never was common in the interior of North America, but a few occur locally in winter from southern Indiana and Illinois to the Gulf coast of Louisiana and Texas. It is more common along the Pacific coast, and winters regularly from southern British Columbia to southern California (Ventura County), and probably one was seen at San Rafael, Lower California. The species is recorded as wintering on Near Island, Alaska, far north of the usual winter home. One was seen January 18, 1904, near Colonia Diaz, Chihuahua, and some years earlier one was killed in the winter at Silao, Guanajuato.

Spring migration.—The northward movement begins in March, as shown by the following dates of arrival: Erie, Pa., March 11, 1897; Williamsport, Pa., March 20, 1905; Deerfield, N. Y., March 13, 1890; Lockport, N. Y., March 20, 1886; Detroit, Mich., March 14, 1905; Delavan, Wis., April 1, 1895, March 31, 1896; Heron Lake, Minn., April 6, 1886, March 31, 1894; Elk River, Minn., April 8, 1886; Fort Collins, Colo., March 16, 1895; Jordan River, Utah, March 10, 1850; St. Michael, Alaska, April 27, 1878; Kowak River, Alaska, May 11, 1899; Fort Simpson, Mackenzie, May 5, 1904; Fort Anderson, Mackenzie, May 18, 1865, and Melville Island, May 31, 1820. One seen near St. John, New Brunswick, April 8, 1882, seems to be the only spring record on the Atlantic coast north of Long Island for the last fifty years.

Since the species breeds to the westward of Hudson Bay and winters commonly on Chesapeake Bay and yet is practically unknown in spring in northeastern North America, it follows that its route in spring migration trends to the northwestward, and it is evident why at this season the species is not uncommon in the region of the Great Lakes and Manitoba.

Most whistling swans leave the United States from the middle to the latter part of April; unusually late birds were seen near Baltimore May 4, 1905, at Williamsport, Pa., May 30, 1901, while nonbreeders have spent the summer on Lake Malheur, Oregon.

Eggs were found at Nulato, Alaska, May 21, somewhat later at the mouth of the Yukon, and about the 1st of June in northern Alaska. The last egg of a set found on Winter Island, Melville Peninsula, was laid June 9, 1822.

Fall migration.—A fine set of records of the arrival of this species in the fall at Alexandria, Va., gives November 6 as the average date for sixteen years, and the birds became common by November 22; the earliest date was October 15, 1901. Near Baltimore, Md., an unusually early bird was seen September 26, 1893. The northern part of Alaska is deserted in early September, and the southern part a month later; few individuals arrive at their winter quarters on the Pacific coast before November.

Olor buccinator (Rich.). Trumpeter Swan.

Breeding range.—The principal summer home of this swan is in the interior of North America from the western shore of Hudson Bay to the Rocky Mountains, and from about latitude 60° to the Arctic Ocean. In early times it probably bred south to Indiana, Wisconsin, Iowa, Nebraska, Montana, and Idaho; it nested in Iowa as late as 1871; in Idaho in 1877; in Minnesota in 1886, and in North Dakota probably for a few years later. It is not probable that at the present time the trumpeter nests anywhere in the United States, and even in Alberta no nests seem to have been found later than 1891. The vast wilderness of but a generation ago is now crossed by railroads and thickly dotted with farms. The species is supposed still to breed in the interior of British Columbia at about latitude 53°. The eggs have been taken at Fort Yukon, and this is the westernmost record of the species.

Winter range.—As the summer home of the trumpeter swan is in the interior, so also is the winter home. The species is not rare south to Texas and remains as far north as it can find open water, sometimes a far as southern Illinois and southern Indiana. During its migrations it occasionally strays to the Atlantic slope (Lincoln, Del., November 9, 1886; Cayuga Lake; Buffalo). Throughout the western mountains of the United States south to Colorado, it is hardly to be considered more than a rare straggler, but on the Pacific coast it is not uncommon in winter from southern British Columbia to southern California (Los Angeles County).

Spring migration.—Early writers on the movements of this species in the northern interior of Canada agree in considering it one of the earliest migrants, arriving before the geese and next after the bald eagle, which is the first spring bird in that region. It is reported to have been seen at Fort Carlton, latitude 52°, March 30. There are no United States records that corroborate this view; the first arrive in southern Iowa, on the average, March 19; at Heron Lake, Minn., the average date of arrival is April 4, earliest March 21, 1889 (a very early spring); other average dates are: Nebraska, March 16; South Dakota, April 2; North Dakota, April 15; Saskatchewan, April 16; British Columbia about April 20. All these dates are later than those which mark the arrival in these districts of the early ducks and geese.

Fall migration.—The trumpeter begins to move south early in September, crosses into the United States the last of that month, and reaches the Gulf of Mexico in Texas about the middle of November. The last remain on the breeding grounds until October, when they are forced away by the gathering ice.

INDEX.

THE LIBRARY OF THE
O AUG 12 1943
UNIVERSITY OF ILLINOIS

www.ingramcontent.com/pod-product-compliance
Lightning Source LLC
Chambersburg PA
CBHW081840280526
45789CB00007B/2521